FORGOTTEN STRUGGLES

African-Americans Confront Racism During the Korean War Era

DR. OTIS ELIOT POPE, JR.

CONTENTS

PREFACE

Roughly fifteen years ago I took a class called Primary Sources at DePaul University, taught by Professor Warren Schultz. The class looked at primary sources as historical documents which shed light on events and revealed deeper meanings about society, culture and politics. During the class, we were assigned a number of readings which looked at the importance of primary sources and how to contextualize and analyze them. The objective of the class was to give students tools to uncover the meaning behind primary sources. The final assessment required each student to go out and find a primary source which had some meaning to that student and write a paper about the cultural, political and/or historical significance of that primary source.

After class was over, I walked to my car, started my engine and began the long drive from Lincoln Park to Olympia Fields. As I drove home, I could not help but think about the assignment. Where would I get a primary source which had some historical meaning which also had some connection to me? How would I design my paper and presentation on that primary source? When I got home, I went straight to bed. I was exhausted, not only because it was late, but also because I was anxious to figure out what type of primary source I could use for the class.

The next morning I went downstairs, made a bowl of oatmeal and a cup of coffee, went outside and retrieved the *Chicago Tribune* from my parents' driveway. As I was reading the paper and eating my breakfast, my mom walked into the kitchen, poured herself a cup of coffee and asked how class was the night before. As I explained my assignment to her, a light bulb went off in my head. Maybe she could help locate a primary source to complete my final project. So, I asked my mom bluntly: "My final assessment for my final Primary Source class requires I get a primary source and analyze it for its historical significance. Do you have any idea where I could get a primary source which fits this requirement?"

She looked at me and said, "Give me a minute." That minute passed, and then another, and still no answer from my mom.

Finally, I asked, "Well, do you have any ideas?"

She said, "Maybe. Your Uncle Kenneth has a collection of letters that he sent to Nanee," — a name we used to affectionately call my grandmother, Thelma Gibson — "from North Africa and Italy during World War II. He keeps them in a shoebox in his room. You might want to call him and see if you can set up a time to go over to his house to look at the letters."

I thought for a minute, and then I thanked her for the advice. I took the number from my mom and called Uncle Kenneth. While I was not particularly close with him, he was always kind to me and I knew he would help if I asked.

We arranged a time for me to go by his house so I could take a look at his letters. After the phone call, I started to work on a list of questions I would ask Uncle Kenneth when I got there.

This was the first time I had been to his house. I would run into him at family gatherings like weddings, funerals and family parties, but I never sat down and talked with him for an extended period of time. Uncle Kenneth lived in the South Shore area in a small, humble brick Georgian house. Georgian homes were simple yet durable and highly utilitarian. On the first floor you had a kitchen, dining room and living room and on the second floor were three small bedrooms. No flash, just the basics.

Uncle Kenneth's house was a reflection of him. He was short, stocky, humble but proud, observant and reserved. He did not say much, but when he did talk, people listened. A graduate of Northwestern University, he had a long, illustrious career with the Internal Revenue Service. He moved up the ranks to eventually become a regional director. Beyond that, Uncle Kenneth was wealthy, though you would never know it just by looking at him. He and one of his wartime buddies, Bill Ball, had quietly invested in IBM before it became a successful business in the early 1980s, and made a fortune. And he was a prominent member of Kappa Alpha Psi, an African-American fraternity, at Northwestern University. (With his support, I joined the Chicago Alumni Chapter of Kappa Alpha Psi in 2004.)

When I rang my uncle's doorbell, my Aunt Mamie, his wife, opened the door. She gave me a warm smile, hugged me and told me to come in. She took my coat, and I sat down in their living room. Moments later, Uncle Kenneth came charging down the stairs. We exchanged greetings. Wasting no time, he said, "Let's get started." I filled him in again on my project and told him I would love to take a look at some of the letters he had written to Nanee during World War II. He got up from his chair and said, "I will be right back," and sprinted up the stairs. A minute later he came back down with a dusty shoebox.

When Uncle Kenneth opened the shoebox, it was almost as though he had opened a time capsule which took us back to the early 1940s. Each letter was still in remarkably good shape given they were written over sixty years before. The stationery the letters were written on was a light brown color and the paper had a crinkly quality, but overall the letters were still in good shape. Uncle Kenneth's penmanship was superb, but there were times when I had trouble reading some of his handwriting, so he helped me interpret some of the letters. As I went through each piece of paper, I stumbled across a letter he wrote to my grandmother on May 8th, 1945, highlighting several aspects of his life as a U.S. soldier. The letter discussed how he spent his leisure time, what challenges he faced in attempting to complete his job, and how he responded to the United States' victory against Germany.

At the beginning of the letter Uncle Kenneth discussed the meaning of "V-E Day" as "another day to me and I thought more of the victory in terms of the lives of men and women and wasted money and material."[1] The tone of the statement struck me as peculiar. The United States had just won a long and bloody war. Yet, he was not celebrating victory over Nazi Germany. Instead, Uncle Kenneth experienced "V-E Day" in a nonchalant and indifferent manner.

When I pressed him on it, Uncle Kenneth began to cry. These were tears of sorrow and pain, and my inquisitive mind had just inadvertently opened a wound. He told me African-Americans died for a country which claimed to stand for liberty and freedom for all, yet the U.S. military at the time was still segregated and Jim Crow laws reigned supreme in the United States. A victory over Nazi Germany meant nothing to him or, in his eyes, to the African-American community.

The theme of racism was not limited to one letter, but was directly highlighted in a number of other letters he wrote. A few days later, on May 13th, 1945, Uncle Kenneth wrote another letter to Nanee where he enclosed a *Stars and Stripes* editorial. The column highlighted the Double V campaign which African-Americans faced during the war. The Double V campaign meant they fought against Nazis and also against overt and covert forms of racism within the U.S. military. Uncle Kenneth wanted

---

[1]   Kenneth Gibson to Thelma Gibson, May 8, 1945, "Kenneth Gibson Letter," Kenneth Gibson's Home

his mother to know he, along with other African-American soldiers, were facing widespread racism within the U.S. military as they sought to serve their country during a time of war.

After numerous meetings with Uncle Kenneth and spending time grappling with the letters, I finally wrote the paper. On the final day of my Primary Source class, each student was required to present their primary source and their paper. When my turn came to present, Professor Schultz listened attentively to my presentation and then looked at the May 13th letter and *Stars and Stripes* editorial.

After the presentation was over, he said, "This letter and editorial piece needs to be in a museum." I took that to mean I did a good job finding a primary source for the assignment. Beyond that, I interpreted what he said as a sign I should continue to learn more about the African-American experience and war. While I did not realize it at the time, Professor Schultz's Primary Source class changed me. It helped me discover a passion I did not know existed within me — a desire to learn more about the African-American experience during war.

After graduating from DePaul, I went back to the classroom to teach for a few years, but I never forgot about that class. Like a fond memory you cannot let go, Professor Schultz's class would linger in my mind, reminding me that my true passion was in researching and writing about the African-American experience during war. Finally, I decided to act on my desire to learn more about the African-American experience. I returned to school to start work on my Ph.D in American History at Loyola University.

When I entered the Ph.D program at Loyola, I immediately sought out historians who focused on war. Professor Theodore Karamanski, a U.S. Public Historian, became a mentor and friend and provided me with some valuable information. As a former Vietnam War veteran, Professor Karamanski was curious about my interest and wanted to help. Sitting in his office one afternoon, filled with pictures, memorabilia and other historical artifacts, he told me, "Eliot, World War II history has been covered by numerous historians. However, you might want to take a look at the African-American experience during The Forgotten War, better known as the Korean War." Like Professor Schultz had done for me at DePaul, Professor Karamanski sparked my curiosity. The African-American experience during the Korean War became my target.

A lot has changed for me since I took Professor Schultz's class fifteen years ago. Uncle Kenneth passed away. I have some gray hair now. I got married to my wonderful wife, Yaneth. I put on a little weight. I do not have the youthful vigor I once had. And I have grown wiser; at least I hope I have. One thing, however, remains the same — a desire to learn about the African-American experience during war and to share that fascination with others. *Forgotten Struggles: African-Americans Confront Racism During the Korean War Era* is a direct result of my love for this topic. I hope the inspirational stories of African-Americans, both those who served during the Korean War and those who fought on their behalf for equality in civil society, will motivate others to learn more about this intriguing yet understudied chapter in American history.

INTRODUCTION

Ensign Jesse Brown took off from the aircraft carrier *Leyte* (CV 33) on December 4th, 1950. Brown's mission provided air support for U.S. Marines and soldiers who were under attack by Chinese soldiers.[2] Flying in a squadron of six Vought F4U Corsairs, his airplane flew over the North Korean coastline at just over one thousand feet above hostile terrain. During the flight, Brown's aircraft suffered mechanical failure, forcing him to make an emergency landing on a snowy hillside in North Korea. Though he survived the landing, Brown's left knee was tangled in a web of metal. Lieutenant Thomas Hudner, his wingman, made a heroic landing next to Brown's aircraft. With no tools to remove Brown's leg from the wreckage, Hudner could not free his fellow soldier. Brown, despite his efforts, eventually slipped into unconsciousness and died.[3] Brown's participation in the Korean War as a Navy pilot was symbolic, as he became the first African-American to fly a U.S. Navy airplane in combat.

---

[2]   Bernard Nalty, *Long Passage to Korea* (Washington D.C.: Naval Historical Center, 2003), v.

[3]   Nalty, *Long Passage to Korea*, v.

Brown's story is sad but heroic. The story hits all the right chords. It is sentimental. It portrays a brave young warrior flying into battle and ultimately losing his life. It highlights the story of a young man paying the ultimate sacrifice to help defend democracy. The story even has a redemptive quality to it. Brown's story challenges the stereotype African-American soldiers were not smart enough to fly airplanes by framing him, rightfully, as a brave, talented young pilot who died for what he believed in. The story also incorporates a theme of racial reconciliation. Hudner, also a Navy pilot and White, making such a valiant effort to save him suggests a friendship had been established between the men.

Brown's story fits in with the broader narrative that Executive Order 9981, which desegregated the U.S. military, brought an end to segregation in the U.S. military. The story creates the illusion solidarity between African-American and White soldiers had finally been achieved, when, in fact, this was not true. Brown's story, while incredibly tragic in some ways and uplifting in others, was exceptional. Some collaboration existed between the races during the Korean War, but a dominant theme of racism and injustice was evident during the war, ensuring African-American and White soldiers would not come together, but would remain apart throughout most of the war.

While racial tensions prevented solidarity from taking hold in the U.S. military between African-American and White soldiers, the Korean War era did witness a blossoming of a more assertive African-American community willing to take on racism both within the U.S. military and within American society. The African-American community launched an attack on racial inequality on three fronts — within civil society, within the U.S. military justice system and within the U.S. military itself during the Korean War. Asa Randolph's advocacy to desegregate the U.S. military, African-American soldiers' preparation for war and service in spite of racism, and Thurgood Marshall's brilliant defense against unjust court-martials garnered real results. As a result of these efforts, a stronger, more energized and cohesive African-American community emerged.

The Korean War was a watershed moment within the civil rights movement. As a result of Randolph's efforts, the U.S. military was technically desegrated, which had numerous implications for African-American soldiers. During the Korean War, African-American soldiers would have an opportunity to prove themselves on the battlefield through hand-to-hand combat with North Korean and Chinese soldiers. The all-Black 24th Infantry, for example, proved they were reliable soldiers despite enduring relentless racism. The African-American community demonstrated it could defend itself against dubious court-martials which sought to undermine their legacy. In doing so, they forged a better future for themselves, their families and, above all, America.

Scholarship on the African-American experience during the Korean War is thin. It often paints with broad brushstrokes, missing key details which were fundamental to the African-American experience. Historiography on the African-American experience during the Korean War is flawed because some of the books embrace what I call the "Kumbaya" theory. The name comes from an African spiritual from the Gullah people of South Carolina. The lyrics to the song are straightforward: *Someone's singing lord, Kumbaya. Someone's crying lord, Kumbaya. Someone's praying lord, Kumbaya, Oh Lord Kumbaya.*[4] The "Kumbaya" theory simply means some historians have embraced a cheery, uplifting narrative rooted in racial reconciliation during the Korean War. These stories look and feel nice, but they often misrepresent the true story of African-Americans during the Korean War.

Bernard Nalty's *Long Passage to Korea* is a perfect example of the "Kumbaya" theory. The book looks at the U.S. military's evolution on racial integration.[5] From African-American participation in the U.S. military during the Revolutionary War to the Civil War and, finally, to the Korean War, the book traces the trajectory of how the U.S. military eventually embraced integration.[6] Although Nalty addresses the Korean War, the conflict is not the centerpiece of the book. Nalty is more concerned with describing how the U.S. military evolved to accept racial inclusion. Consequently, the Korean War is used in this book as the crowning achievement of the implementation of this policy.

---

[4] "When Did 'Kumbaya' Become Such A Bad Thing?," *National Public Radio*, August 4, 2020, https://www.npr.org/2012/01/13/145059502/when-did-kumbaya-become-such-a-bad-thing.

[5] Bernard Nalty, *Long Passage to Korea* (Washington D.C: Naval Historical Center, 2003), 46.

[6] Nalty, *Long Passage to Korea*, v.

Nalty argues racial reconciliation was achieved through the creation of the Fahy committee and Executive Order 9981. The book examines Executive Order 9981, which banned discrimination in the U.S. military, as a way to highlight President Truman's commitment to desegregating the U.S. military.[7] Additionally, Nalty suggests the U.S. Navy aimed to increase the number of African-Americans within the naval force through the creation of the Fahy Committee, a panel which sought to find solutions to best integrate African-Americans into the U.S. military.[8] As Nalty wrote, the Fahy Committee found "there were no programs to recruit or commission African-Americans."[9] As a result of this commission and Executive Order 9981, Nalty asserts the Korean War represented the apex for the U.S. military's stance on racial inclusion. While Nalty's book is inspirational, it creates the illusion the Korean War was in some way a triumph over racism and segregation within the U.S. military, even though evidence suggests otherwise.

Not all historiography frames the Korean War as a watershed moment in race relations. Edward Posey's *The U.S. Army's First, Last, and Only All-Black Rangers* highlights the military exploits of this select group of highly trained African-American soldiers. Posey's book examines how African-American Rangers fought simultaneously against North Korean soldiers and racism within the U.S. military. Influential military leaders like General Edward Almond, an avowed racist and staunch supporter of

---

[7] Ibid., 28.

[8] Ibid., 30.

[9] Ibid.

segregation, opposed the integration of African-Americans. As General Almond put it, "When you say you have to have ten percent Negroes (in the Army), you are lowering the combat efficiency of the Army."[10] General Almond believed African-American soldiers weakened the U.S. military. Posey refutes this point. He argues the Rangers persevered on the battlefield. Through their service, the Rangers broke down stereotypes and proved African-Americans were first-class soldiers. Posey claims the objective of Rangers was to "provide protection for the aid station, provide security on the northern flank of the military police outpost, and hunt down guerillas in the area who could raid the main supply route."[11] The Rangers exceeded expectations and, in so doing, brought honor to their fighting unit and to the African-American community.

Posey reveals how racism affected the rescue efforts for this elite African-American fighting unit. The sacrifice they made is chronicled in the death of one particular member whose body was riddled with bullet wounds. "His intestines were spread out on the ground."[12] Later, the Rangers attempted to get their comrade on a helicopter to take him to get medical attention, but personnel refused. In response to this rejection, one Ranger put a .45 caliber handgun to the neck of the helicopter pilot and "informed him Kirk was going in that chopper, or else!"[13] In this case, African-American soldiers were not considered valuable enough

---

[10] Edward Posey, *The U.S. Army's First, Last, and Only All Black Rangers* (New York: Savas Beati, 2009), 60.

[11] Posey, *The U.S. Army's First, Last, and Only All Black Rangers*, 36.

[12] Ibid., 104.

[13] Ibid.

to be picked up by a helicopter for medical attention. Nonetheless, African-American soldiers found ways to exercise agency.

Like Posey's work, *Firefight at Yechon* by Lieutenant Colonel Charles Bussey frames African-American contributions during the Korean War as a positive. Colonel Bussey's first-person account highlights his experience as an officer in the U.S. Army in the Korean War.[14] In his words, "I have been haunted by the generalized and not completely objective portrayals and comparisons of how African-American soldiers performed in the Korean War."[15] African-Americans were stereotyped as lacking courage and were deemed unreliable.

Colonel Bussey confronts these notions of African-American inferiority within the U.S. military in several ways. First, he suggests the accolades African-American soldiers received during the Vietnam War validated their worthiness as soldiers during the Korean War. As Colonel Bussey wrote, "If we were so poor then, why did African-American soldiers get such high marks in the Vietnam War, only fifteen years after Korea?"[16] Second, Colonel Bussey maintains the reason African-American soldiers did not serve with honor in the Korean War was largely because the U.S. military did not appreciate their contributions to the war effort.[17] When African-American soldiers "received respect" from the U.S. military, then African-American troops responded by being

---

[14]   Charles Bussey, *Firefight at Yechon* (New York: Macmillan, 1991), xiv.

[15]   Bussey, *Firefight at Yechon*, 261.

[16]   Ibid.

[17]   Ibid.

better, more responsible soldiers.[18] Hence, Colonel Bussey's book counters previous literature which cast African-American soldiers as inferior relative to White soldiers.

Not all books suggested African-Americans found success in the Korean War. Some, in fact, imply the opposite. William Bowers, William Hammond and George MacGarrigle's book entitled *Black Soldier, White Army: The 24th Infantry Regiment in Korea* portray the African-American experience as a setback to the full integration of African-American soldiers into the U.S. military. Bowers, Hammond and MacGarrigle achieve this by highlighting the failures of the 24th Infantry, an all-Black fighting unit.[19] The book argues institutional racism limited the military effectiveness of the 24th.[20] A variety of factors, including structural racism, created the circumstances for the 24th to underperform.[21] According to Bowers, Hammond and MacGarrigle, the unit failed because of "an aggressive enemy, inadequate equipment, inexperience at all levels, leadership failures high and low, casualties among key personnel, and a lack of bonding and cohesion in some units."[22] Simply put, the book suggests systemic issues embedded within the U.S. military were key to the 24th's poor performance on the battlefields of Korea.[23]

---

[18]   Ibid.

[19]   William T. Bowers, William M. Hammond and George L. MacGarrigle, *Black Soldier, White Army: The 24th Infantry Regiment in Korea* (Washington D.C.: Center of Military History, 1996), iii.

[20]   Bowers, Hammond and MacGarrigle, *Black Soldier, White Army: The 24th Infantry Regiment in Korea*, iii.

[21]   Ibid., 267.

[22]   Ibid.

[23]   Ibid.

Bowers, Hammond and MacGarrigle's book differs from other works on the subject matter because it does not frame African-American contributions in the U.S. military in a positive light. In fact, it presents the opposite by indicating African-American soldiers, particularly in the 24th, did poorly in battle due to a combination of external factors. By doing this, the book provides a critical piece to the larger narrative of the African-American experience during the Korean War by drawing a direct link between African-American performance on the battlefield and their treatment by the U.S. military. In spite of President Truman's Executive Order 9981 which integrated the U.S. military, African-American soldiers still suffered from poor treatment by their superiors. Bowers, Hammond and MacGarrigle challenge the narrative put forth by works like Bernard Nalty's *Long Passage to Korea* which claims African-American integration into the U.S. military was smooth. Instead, the book implies the integration of African-American soldiers into the U.S. military was tumultuous at best.

African-Americans in the U.S. military, just like in American society, were treated poorly, often disrespected and undervalued. The dismantling of the 24th, an African-American fighting unit, reveals the ups and downs, curves and twists all African-American servicemen faced in the U.S. military. They were revered in certain circumstances and ostracized in others. They were embraced for their heroism and valiant fighting efforts in certain circles, while, at the same time, vilified for not fighting effectively by other factions within the U.S. Armed Forces. Some won awards for bravery, while others were court-martialed for dereliction of duty.

In spite of the 24th's controversial reputation, which it did not deserve, the 24th did serve with distinction over the seventy-five years of its existence. The 38th and 41st Infantries, which were the predecessors of the 24th, were established in 1866.[24] The men who made up the 38th and 41st were a mixture of trained and untrained men. Some came from the North, while others came from the South.[25] Eventually, the 38th and 41st were disbanded and reorganized as the 24th in October 1869.[26]

Over the course of the next decade, the 24th fought against groups of Indian raiders, escorted supply trains, and provided protection for railroad and wagon road construction teams. The 24th even guarded supply lines and water holes. Beyond that, the 24th played a key role in preventing the Indian warrior Victorio, from the Apache tribe, from entering Texas from Mexico.[27] In fact, two soldiers from the 24th were even awarded the Medal of Honor after protecting an Army paymaster during a robbery.[28] Major Joseph Wham, the paymaster, stated, "I served in the infantry during the entire Civil War… in sixteen major battles, but I never witnessed better fighting than shown by these colored soldiers."[29]

---

[24] Ibid., 5.
[25] Ibid.
[26] Ibid.
[27] Ibid., 6.
[28] Ibid., 7.
[29] Ibid.

In spite of their military exploits, racism ensured the 24th was not given full credit for their military exploits. The U.S. military mirrored societal norms and behavioral patterns within American society. Like a wildfire which spread uncontrollably, racism between the 1870s to 1900s infected every aspect of American life. As southern Democrats took power, they passed restrictive voting registration and electoral laws. Additionally, they passed "separate but equal" laws which guaranteed Whites and African-Americans were set apart from one another.[30] At this same time, a campaign to dismantle the 24th emerged. The movement originated from the idea that African-American soldiers were not good soldiers. As one commentator put it, "The Negroes are not self-sustaining."[31] The person later went on to say, "They have no mechanics, no clerks, very few of them know how to read and write."[32] In other words, the pundit suggested African-American soldiers were useless, and, more to the point, should be removed from military service.

In reality, the men of the 24th were neither cowards or useless. They were soldiers who took pride in their work. In 1896, for example, the 24th was sent to Salt Lake City. Salt Lake City residents were distraught. To address their concerns, they sent a group of people to Washington to protest. The anger residents of Salt Lake City exhibited towards the men of the 24th was rooted in racism. They did not want African-American men in their communities. They believed they would rape, steal, and pillage

---

[30] Ibid.

[31] Ibid.

[32] Ibid.

the city. The 24th, however, proved them wrong. They were professional and displayed concern for their community. In fact, a newspaper from Salt Lake City even made a public apology to the 24th.[33] As the members of the 24th prepared to head off to fight in the Spanish-American War, the people of Salt Lake City came out to wish them well.[34]

In the late 19th century, the United States was an emerging power. Its economy was growing at a rapid pace and the country's military was formidable. Yet, the United States wanted more. It wanted an empire. It desired political and economic influence over territory outside its borders. European countries such as England, France and Germany controlled large swaths of land throughout Africa, Southeast Asia and North America. By controlling these territories, they extracted valuable minerals and resources, including palm oil, diamonds and cooper – for financial gain and, beyond that, to compete for world supremacy.

Of the numerous European powers which participated in this high-stakes game, Spain's empire by the late 19th century was the most fragile. In April 1895, a rebellion broke out on the island of Cuba. The United States closely monitored the situation because it had strong economic and real estate interests in Cuba. To accommodate growing alarm in the United States media, President McKinley sent the USS *Maine*, a second-class destroyer, to Cuba on January 24th, 1898.[35] After negotiations between Spain and the United States took place, Spain reluctantly let the U.S.

---

[33]   Ibid., 8.

[34]   Ibid.

[35]   Jerome Tuccille, *The Roughest Riders* (Chicago: Chicago Review Press, 2015), 19.

Navy send the armored cruiser to Cuba. The USS *Maine* was a large ship. It measured 324 feet and four inches in length. The ship was divided into 214 watertight compartments. It was relatively fast. It could generate nine thousand horsepower and reach a maximum speed of seventeen knots. Moreover, the boat had significant firepower. The battleship had four ten-inch guns, two gun turrets, six six-inch guns, and seven rapid-fire six-pounders. It even had the ability to fire torpedoes with four torpedo tubes on its side.[36]

When the USS *Maine* arrived in Havana, it anchored in the harbor. Its crew kept a close watch on the island of Cuba. Three weeks after it arrived, on Feb. 15th, 1898, the USS *Maine* blew up in a gigantic fireball. American newspapers sensationalized the event by blaming the Spanish for the explosion, though evidence suggested it was a result of a mechanical problem onboard the ship. As a result of the explosion, Cuban exiles and the American press were calling for the Spanish to leave Cuba. Newspapers depicted Spain's leaders as evil and inhumane individuals. Powerful newspaper owners like William Hearst, owner of the *San Francisco Examiner*, called for war. As a consequence, Hearst's demands, a public outcry over the massive explosion which sank the USS *Maine*, and American real estate and economic interests together resulted in the United States declaring war on Spain.[37]

---

[36]   Tuccille, *The Roughest Riders*, 19 – 20.

[37]   Ibid., 20 – 21.

One of the most powerful advocates for going to war with Spain was Theodore Roosevelt, President McKinley's Assistant Secretary of the Navy and the future President of the United States. Described by some as outgoing and forthright and others as intelligent with a hint of recklessness, Roosevelt was an opportunistic politician looking for a chance to elevate his national stature. Roosevelt jumped at the opportunity to serve in the U.S. military at the outset of the Spanish-American War. Before the war, Roosevelt created the Rough Riders, a group of cowboys and men from blue blood families from New England. Roosevelt would lead these men into battle against the Spanish in Cuba. The Rough Riders, coupled with the 24th, referred to by many as the Buffalo Soldiers, executed America's new vigorous foreign policy on the world stage at the turn of the century.

While many gave the Rough Riders credit for helping to win the Spanish-American War, African-American soldiers, including men from the 24th, were, in fact, the true heroes of the conflict. The selection of African-Americans to fight in the Spanish-American War was grounded in scientific racism. Major General Miles reasoned, "The Negro is better able to withstand the Cuban climate than the White man."[38] In other words, General Miles believed African-Americans were genetically equipped to deal with the hot, blistering sun and humidity in Cuba. As a result of this appalling racist logic, African-American soldiers were sent to Cuba to fight.

---

[38]   Ibid., 31.

Although a number of key battles were fought during the Spanish-American War, the battle of Kettle Hill and San Juan Hill are arguably the most famous. During these clashes, American troops had a number of disadvantages as they fought against the Spanish. First, they had old rifles which gave off smoke, while the Spanish had smokeless rifles. The fume emitting rifles the Americans used let the Spanish know exactly where they were on the battlefield.[39] Secondly, the Spanish had the high ground, making it easy for them to fight off American troops charging up the hills.[40] As Roosevelt and his men went up Kettle Hill, bullets rained down on them from Spanish soldiers. Many Rough Riders were either wounded or killed. Just as the Rough Riders were making it up Kettle Hill, African-American soldiers from the 24th, who were fighting alongside Roosevelt and his men, made it to the top of the bluff.

After the Rough Riders and soldiers from the 24th took Kettle Hill, they charged down the slope and then went up San Juan Hill, joining the other Buffalo Soldiers who were led by Major "Black Jack" Pershing. Meanwhile, Roosevelt and the Rough Riders, who suffered heavy losses, stayed behind. At the same time, Buffalo Soldiers engaged with enemy combatants on San Juan Hill.[41] When they got to the top of the ridge, they planted the American flag. Ironically, Roosevelt did not get up to the top of San Juan Hill until the fighting was over. When Roosevelt finally made

---

[39] Ibid., 123.

[40] Ibid., 105.

[41] Ibid., 152 – 153.

it to the top of the hill's crest after the fighting had stopped, he was greeted by seven handpicked reporters.

The seven reporters played a pivotal role in shaping the narrative of the Rough Riders. Roosevelt paid close attention to Richard Davis, giving him stories which were not available to others, anticipating these narrative accounts would eventually land on the front pages of the *New York Herald*. John Dunning wrote for the Associated Press, which made him valuable to Roosevelt because it had a massive distribution. Kenneth Harris wrote for the *Chicago Record* and praised Roosevelt's every move. Edward Marshall and Stephen Crane were both brilliant writers who Roosevelt could rely on to frame the Rough Riders and, above all, himself in a positive light. Casper Whitney from *Harper's* was a competent professional with a good reputation. Finally, Frederic Remington, an artist, was useful because he worked for the powerful newspaper magnate William Hearst. Remington's illustrations of the war would be showcased in the *New York Journal*.[42] As a result, Roosevelt's control of the narrative of the Spanish-American War ensured he and the Rough Riders would be portrayed as heroic warriors who fought bravely and emerged victorious in the battles which took place on San Juan and Kettle Hill. At the same token, Buffalo Soldiers, comprised of African-American soldiers from the 24th and 25th Infantries, participation in these bloody encounters was written off as inconsequential.

---

[42]   Ibid., 94 – 95.

In reality, Roosevelt was no hero. Instead, he was a clever politician who used his power to manipulate the historical narrative of the Spanish-American War for political ends.

Roosevelt's complicity in devaluing African-American soldiers' role in the Spanish-American War was not the only racist slight they endured. Even Major Pershing, the famous U.S. military leader who praised African-American soldiers and their military prowess during the war, criticized them after the Spanish-American War. In a French military mission in Europe on August 17th, 1918, he advised French officers, "We must not eat with them, must not shake hands or seek to talk or meet with them outside the requirements of military service." He later went on to say, "We must not commend too highly African-American troops, particularly in the presence of Americans…. Americans become greatly incensed at any public expression of intimacy between White women with African-American men."[43] Major Pershing's words stung. They were indicative of the incredible amount of discrimination African-American soldiers faced.

Racism did not start nor did it stop after the Spanish-American War. On August 23rd, 1917 on a hot, muggy night a riot erupted in the streets of Houston, Texas. The bloody rampage underscored the dangers associated with the pervasive racism African-American soldiers encountered. Before the mutiny, African-American soldiers from the 24th were transferred to Camp Logan, located near Houston, Texas. While stationed at Camp Logan, African-American soldiers guarded the construction site

---

[43]   Ibid., 244.

of a new training camp. As African-American soldiers poured into the Houston area, the surrounding White community's disdain for them grew. White Houston residents frequently verbally assaulted African-American soldiers from the 24th. As one local White person put it, "A nigger is a nigger, and … his status is not effected (sic) by the uniform he wears."[44] In addition to the barrage of racial insults they experienced, the 24th's resentment of Jim Crow laws and the brutal and vicious manner in which Houston police officers treated them ignited an uncontrollable rage which left dead bodies in its wake. During the riot, over one hundred soldiers from the 24th took up arms and marched into Houston. In the course of two hours, sixteen Whites were killed and twelve others injured. Likewise, five African-American soldiers from the 24th, including one who committed suicide, died.[45] After the riot, dozens of African-American soldiers from the 24th were imprisoned. And, nineteen African-American soldiers were hung.

Disrespect towards African-American soldiers would continue well after the Houston riot of 1917. During World War II, aside from a few exceptions such as the Tuskegee Airmen and 761st Tank Battalion, most African-Americans did not fight in the war. The 24th, for example, was relegated to guarding supply lines and delivering weapons and food to White soldiers on the frontline during World War II. They were deemed

---

[44]   William T. Bowers, William M. Hammond and George L. MacGarrigle, *Black Soldier, White Army: The 24th Infantry Regiment in Korea* (Washington D.C.: Center of Military History, 1996), 14.

[45]   Bowers, Hammond and MacGarrigle, *Black Soldier, White Army: The 24th Infantry Regiment in Korea*, 14.

not smart enough, not courageous enough, not responsible enough to fight battle-hardened Japanese and German soldiers. Likewise, some Whites were hesitant to allow African-Americans to fight, fearing they might take up arms against them. In effect, the vast majority of African-Americans were not able to showcase their skills as soldiers on the battlefield.

The Korean War was different. African-American soldiers would not be consigned to the periphery of the U.S. military. They would take center stage. Due to manpower shortages within the U.S. military, the Korean War gave the 24th an opportunity to prove itself. They fought alongside other all White infantry units. African-American soldiers were given a chance to demonstrate their manhood by serving their country in battle. The symbolism of the all-Black 24th serving in combat areas sent a shock wave throughout American society. Newspapers and magazines took note of their every move. In turn, the 24th was analyzed and dissected in ways that other infantry regiments were not. In spite of the scrutiny, the 24th fought just as well as their White brethren, bringing honor to their community and, above all, to the United States.

Forgotten Soldiers: African-Americans Confronted Racism During the Korean War Era is unique within historiography on African-Americans and the Korean War. The book rejects the notion racial reconciliation was a byproduct of the Korean War, while arguing African-American soldiers performed well, not poorly, during the "police action." The book asserts racial coexistence, not racial harmony, emerged as a defining characteristic of the relationship between White and African-American soldiers during the conflict. White and African-American soldiers fought together towards the end of the war, but there was no moment where tensions between African-American and White soldiers instantly melted away. Genuine, meaningful relationships between African-American and White soldiers often were not established. There was no point in which African-American and White soldiers hugged each other, declared racism finally over and skipped off into the sunset. Instead, African-American soldiers and White soldiers learned how to collaborate with each other to achieve a common goal.

Additionally, the book demonstrates, despite experiencing debilitating racism on a daily basis, African-American soldiers delivered on their promise to defend democracy and stop the spread of communism in Korea. In doing so, they served their country with honor and dignity. They won numerous medals which underscored their bravery and courage under fire. And, they helped the U.S. military secure key victories at the Battle of Yechon and the Pusan Perimeter. African-American soldiers fought and, in some cases, died like every other soldier in Korea. Through their efforts, African-American troops emerged from the Korean War more confident and self-assured.

Forgotten Soldiers: African-Americans Confronted Racism During the Korean War Era is a story of redemption. It is a story of African-American solidarity, not interracial unity. The book does not frame African-American soldiers achieving success on the battlefield in a linear manner like Lieutenant Colonel Bussey's *Firefight at Yechon* which highlights the heroics of the 77th Engineer Combat Company. The book provides a more nuanced account of the African-American experience during the Korean War era. It emphasizes how the African-American community waged war in civil society, within the U.S. military justice system and on the battlefields of Korea to make their dream of equality for all a reality.

Forgotten Soldiers: African-Americans Confronted Racism During the Korean War Era uses a hybrid top-down and bottom-up method to illuminate a story which has until recently existed in a dark, desolate corner designated for the Korean War within historiography. Specifically, the book showcases the courageousness and perseverance of servicemen such as Ensign Jesse Brown, Curtis Morrow, Roy Dell Johnson and James Williams during the Korean War. Likewise, the book explains how activist such as Asa Randolph and Thurgood Marshall had a direct impact on the lives of countless African-American soldiers who served during the Korean War era. It is this unique combination of soldiers, a civil rights icon and a gifted legal scholar, all working together that would be the catalyst for African-Americans securing their legal rights with the U.S. Armed Forces and, more broadly, American society.

Forgotten Soldiers: African-Americans Confronted Racism During the Korean War Era is broken into six chapters. Chapter one examines how

Asa Randolph, often described as the godfather of the civil rights move-ment, usage of political and social power encouraged President Truman to issue Executive Order 9981, which in theory ended segregation in the U.S. military. Chapter two explores how African-Americans prepared for war and examines the racism they encountered during basic training. Chapter three surveys the range of challenges African-American soldiers faced during combat, including various forms of racism, questionable leadership, frigid weather conditions and battle-hardened North Korean and Chinese soldiers. The chapter also delves into how African-American soldiers revealed at different moments on the battlefield a compassion for others, the capacity to ruthlessly kill and a deep, uncompromising faith in God through their religious piety.

Chapter four shifts from the theatre of war in Korea to the court-rooms of the U.S. military legal system. The chapter concentrates on Thurgood Marshall, a civil rights attorney, and his effort to defend the reputations and, in some instances, lives of African-American soldiers who faced court-martials. Chapter five investigates the implications of the Korean War on the psychology, self-worth, racial consciousness, social awareness and employability of African-American Korean War veterans. Finally, chapter six scrutinizes how a distorted portrayal of the all-Black 24th Infantry's combat performance has misrepresented the real contribution the fighting unit made to the war effort. In particular, the chapter explains how this manipulation of the truth was used as a pretext to abruptly disband the 24th midway thru the Korean War. The chapter concludes with an analysis on how the African-American community can learn from the struggles its forebearers have faced during The Forgotten War to forge a brighter future for themselves and America.

A central component to *Forgotten Struggles: African-Americans Confront Racism During the Korean War Era* is addressing the U.S. military's treatment of the 24th. The infantry's demise during the Korean War was tragic. It was a fighting unit which had the honor, or rather the dishonor, of being the only infantry in U.S. military history to ever be terminated. Even so, the enactment of Executive Order 9981 meant the fate of the 24th was sealed. With the U.S. military slowly moving towards integrating African-American soldiers into the U.S. Armed Forces, it was only a matter of time before the 24th would be decommissioned.

Nevertheless, the U.S. military's timing to dissolve the 24th was problematic. The decision to disband the 24th on October 1st, 1951, which was roughly the halfway point of the Korean War, was offensive because it took place during the war and not after an armistice had been reached between North and South Korea. Consequently, the 24th was subjected to unnecessary ridicule and embarrassment, which invariably spilled over and onto the African-American community because it was a fighting unit which was comprised exclusively of African-American soldiers. The decision to terminate the 24th during the Korean War signaled to African-Americans and Whites at home and abroad that African-American soldiers were not capable of fighting on their own. It reaffirmed racist stereotypes that

African-American soldiers were not smart enough, responsible enough or courageous enough to serve their country in a fighting unit which was designated for African-American soldiers.

Further, the choice to break up the 24th during the war reeked of White saviorism. Many White commanding officers believed African-American soldiers were inherently inferior to White soldiers. To improve the quality of African-American soldiers, some White officers believed they were obligated to *rescue* African-American soldiers from their innate ineptitude. White soldiers would be required to serve as role models for African-American soldiers. They would need to show African-American soldiers how to engage in combat with enemy combatants. They would be required to teach them how to be responsible servicemen. They would have to demonstrate to African-American soldiers how to be courageous warriors.

Of course, this was a slap in the face to every African-American serviceman who served during the Korean War because it suggested they were not capable of being strong, independent soldiers. The time, energy and dedication all African-American soldiers invested in preparing for war meant nothing to the U.S. military. No matter how hard they worked, they would always be perceived as less than equals to their White counterparts in the U.S. military. This anger towards the U.S. military could have been avoided if the 24th was quietly dissolved after a cease-fire was reached between North and South Korea.

Ironically, at the outset of the Korean War, the 24th was praised for their professionalism and courage. The 24th's stellar performance at the battle of Yechon, one of the first major battles of the Korean War, was a testimony to the quality training they received and, above all, to their formidable combat skills. White newspapers ran stories lauding the 24th's professionalism. African-American reporters praised their heroic actions as they engaged in armed combat against enemy combatants. Things would soon change. Within a short period, the North Korean People's Army (NKPA), with help from the Chinese People's Volunteer Army (PVA), made adjustments. They began winning battles against South Korean, US and NATO forces. North Korean and Chinese forces started to turn the tide of the war.

Consequently, the U.S. military was now on the defensive. Just as this was happening, the 24th's reputation began to deteriorate. The 24th went from being praised as dependable protectors of democracy to vilified as incompetent soldiers who could not function without oversight from White commanding officers. In fact, some U.S. military leaders determined the U.S. Armed Forces were underperforming solely because the 24th was not performing well on the battlefield. Regardless of the combat performance of White soldiers during the war, the 24th was largely blamed for the U.S. military's abysmal performance against well trained, intelligent and highly motivated North Korean and Chinese soldiers at the beginning of the Korean War. The 24th became the perfect scapegoat.

Forgotten Soldiers: African-Americans Confront Racism During the Korean War Era seeks to reframe how African-American soldiers are portrayed within historiography. The book suggests the African-American community pushed for social and political change before and during the Korean War era, both within American society and the U.S. military. In doing so, they became masters of their own fate. Men like Asa Randolph, Thurgood Marshall, Curtis Morrow, Ensign Jesse Brown, James Lacy, James Williams and others fought for African-Americans to not only have a chance to serve their country, but to also be granted the respect they deserved for putting their lives on the line to preserve democracy in Korea. This book aims to give these unsung heroes of the Korean War an opportunity to tell their stories on their terms. They will no longer remain silent. Their voices will finally be heard.

CHAPTER 1
Asa Randolph

Prior to Ensign Jesse Brown earning his wings as the first African-American Navy pilot and before the 24th Infantry was disbanded, Asa Randolph's civic activism laid the groundwork for the eventual desegregation of the U.S. military. Considered by some to be the godfather of the civil rights movement, Randolph helped craft the agenda for the civil rights movement in the 1930s and 1940s. He amassed a number of key victories which moved the African-American community closer to securing full citizenship. Through his civic engagement, Randolph confronted two American Presidents to secure rights for African-Americans pertaining to defense contracts and the desegregation of the U.S. Armed Forces. In fact, Randolph's efforts eventually led to President Truman issuing Executive Order 9981, which abolished discrimination based on race, creed, color or religion in the U.S. military. Thus, Randolph's efforts created the circumstances for African-American soldiers to prove themselves as capable soldiers during the Korean War.

Randolph was born on April 15th, 1889 to James and Elizabeth Randolph in Crescent City, Florida, a small town located between two lakes, Crescent Lake and Lake Stella.[46] The small town featured large palm trees, hot and sticky humidity and beautiful sunsets. Randolph's family would later move to Jacksonville, Florida, a thriving railroad hub and home to large, vibrant African-American communities located in Brooklyn, Sugarville, Turkeyvilla and Lavilla. Lawyers and dishwashers, doctors and cleaning ladies, all lived, worked and prayed together in these tight-knit communities. This concentration of African-Americans within these communities was a source of strength.

Randolph grew up in a time where racism was inextricably tied into the fabric of American society. Jacksonville, Florida was no exception to this fact. Jim Crow laws effected every aspect of the lives of African-Americans.[47] It curtailed where they could live and whether or not they could own a home. It limited the quality and type of education they received. It controlled the caliber of health care available to African-Americans. Randolph, however, was shielded from racism by his family and his church.[48] As a byproduct of being sequestered in his home, his bond with his family strengthened and his religious faith deepened. Through his engagement with his parents and siblings, a steady dose of confidence, ambition and hope was drip feed into Randolph. His faith in God

---

[46] Cornelius L. Bynum, *A. Philip Randolph and the Struggle for Civil Rights* (Chicago: University of Illinois Press, 2010), 157.

[47] Bynum, *A. Philip Randolph and the Struggle for Civil Rights*, 4.

[48] Ibid., 5.

provided him with a set of principles and values which shaped his moral compass. These attributes would come in handy when Randolph would challenge powerful organizations and institutions rooted in systematic racism.

James, Randolph's father, left a lasting impression on his son. James had a strong sense of racial pride.[49] A tailor and minister by trade, James had multiple jobs. He was a proud man who loved to work hard, provide for his family and to serve God.[50] James' convictions were put to the test when he learned a White mob was about to lynch an African-American man.[51] Lynching of African-American men usually occurred over the breaking of unspoken but established social norms in the South — an African-American man flirting with a White woman or an African-American entrepreneur who became too successful for Whites to tolerate or a simple petty theft — could lead to an African-American man swinging from a tree with his penis and testicles shoved into his mouth. White men performed these atrocious acts because they believed they were protecting their culture, way of life and the purity of White women.

Luckily for the man, this horrific event did not take place. His lynching did not occur. James ensured the man would live another day. James, after learning a crowd of White people had gathered in downtown Jacksonville to witness a lynching, took it upon himself to confront the crowd

---

[49]   Ibid., 4.
[50]   "A. Philip Randolph," AFL – CIO, accessed December 27th, 2021, https://aflcio.org/about/history/labor-history-people/asa-philip-randolph.
[51]   Ibid.

with a loaded gun. He demanded the White mob free the man immediately. They reluctantly loosened the noose from around the man's neck and took it off. Then, they handed him over to James. Through this heroic act, James gave his son a powerful lesson. It taught Randolph he had a moral obligation to do what was right even if it meant putting his life in danger. It instructed Randolph how to embrace his community and to love his ethnicity. More than that, it demonstrated to Randolph strong African-American men were not impotent but could fight back. They could defend themselves and, if necessary, they too could exact revenge.

James' actions were in stark contrast to what White society said he could or could not do. African-American men were expected to be subservient, not deviant and assertive. They were expected to *stay in their lane*. They were supposed to take the punishment and humiliation. It was a survival mechanism. If you remained quiet, you just might live another day. James did not play the role which White society had ascribed to him. He was something more. He showcased for Randolph an African-American form of masculinity which would not be neutered, compromised or intimidated by White supremacy. He fought back.

James did more than model for Randolph on how to stand up for himself and for his community in the face of adversity. He used storytelling to teach valuable lessons to his children on how to resist racial oppression in all its forms. James told his children about Harriet Tubman's fearlessness in the face of danger. He described to his children how she disguised herself as a field hand by walking with chickens when she first escaped from slavery.[52] Later, he explained how Tubman went back to the South and escorted countless African-Americans on the Underground Railroad to freedom in Canada. He told them about how Frederick Douglass fought back against Mr. Covey, a slave-breaker who specialized in crushing the will of slaves. James described to his children how Douglass successfully defended himself against Mr. Covey's brutality. In doing so, Douglass reaffirmed his sense of self-worth. He described to them how Douglass escaped from slavery by disguising himself as a sailor and boarding a train for New York.[53] Once free, James explained in detail how Douglass slowly remade himself into a powerful, influential abolitionist, orator, author, newspaper editor and statesman.[54]

James told his children about the bloody slave rebellion led by Nat Turner which sent shockwaves throughout southern states. The rebellion left sixty White people dead and unleashed hysteria throughout the South.[55] James' rendition of Turner's prophetic vision while working in his master's field mesmerized Randolph. "The serpent is lucent. Christ laid down the yoke for the sins of man and you shall take it up to fight against the serpent. The time is near when the first shall be last and the last shall be first."[56] The message was clear. African-Americans are worthy of being

---

[52]   Cornelius L. Bynum, *A. Philip Randolph and the Struggle for Civil Rights* (Chicago: University of Illinois Press, 2010), 157. 4.

[53]   Bynum, *A. Philip Randolph and the Struggle for Civil Rights*, 4.

[54]   Ibid.

[55]   Ibid.

[56]   Ibid.

free. Jesus has given the community tools to fight back against the serpent of racial oppression. Most importantly, God commands African-Americans to use these devices to fight for their freedom.

These African-American protagonists became role models for Randolph to live up to in life. They were points of reference within the constellation of narratives of African-Americans resisting the brutal, inhuman system of slavery. Randolph believed if he wanted to make a difference he must exhibit Tubman's bravery, embody Douglass' tenacity and embrace Turner's commitment for equality no matter the consequences. These individuals were not mere mortals to Randolph. They were angels sent from heaven to lead their people to the promised land, just as Moses led the Israelites from the bondage of slavery in Egypt. They were warriors who took on White supremacy in hopes of liberating their people. These stories were like seeds buried in the fertile soil of Randolph's subconscious mind that, once watered and given sunlight, would sprout into ideas, thoughts and actions which informed his behavior.

Randolph's racial awareness was reaffirmed through his early childhood experiences working on the railroad. At fourteen, he was able to secure employment as a water boy on the railroad.[57] Randolph desperately wanted to be a man, and believed getting a job would help him achieve that goal. He believed finding employment would force him out of his protective bubble, making him stronger, wiser and smarter. The job was a learning experience for Randolph, though not quite in the way he

---

[57]   Ibid., 21.

expected. While working as a water boy did make him more responsible, it also gave him a firsthand experience with racism. As Randolph and his fellow coworkers were working, their boss sat down with a loaded rifle and watched them attentively like a hawk eyeing his prey. The experience was emblematic of the unequal power dynamic between Whites and African-Americans.[58] The White man with the gun served as a warning — do your job or you will be punished with violence. While neither Randolph nor his fellow African-American workers were hurt, the message this White man sent to them was laced with racist undertones.

The books Randolph read also shaped his lens on race. Among them, W.E.B. Dubois's *The Souls of Black Folk* left a lasting impression on him. Published in 1903, *The Souls of Black Folk* highlighted the struggles African-Americans faced against racism within the United States. DuBois believed African-American civil rights were connected to social rights.[59] Like salt is to pepper, DuBois reasoned you could not have one without the other. DuBois further argued being a poor person was horrible, but paled in comparison to being someone from an impoverished race, especially in a country as prosperous as the United States.[60] The combination of race and poverty created a kind of hell on earth for African-Americans, relegating them to a life of despair and struggle. DuBois's *The Souls of Black Folk* provided Randolph with a heightened racial consciousness and, above all, informed his civic and social activism later in life.

---

[58] Ibid., 21.

[59] Ibid., 28.

[60] W.E.B. Dubois, *Souls of Black Folks* (New York: Bantam Books, 1945), 11.

Finally, Randolph's participation within the church shaped his perspective on race within America. Christianity in the early 19th century played a critical role in the African-American community. It provided African-Americans with spiritual nourishment and it gave them a sense of community. Stories like the Garden of Eden, which chronicled the story of Adam getting tricked into eating an apple from the forbidden tree, taught Randolph about the benefits of resisting temptation. Other stories such as David, a future King of Israel, defeating the Philistine Goliath informed him on how to have courage in the face of adversity. The Ten Commandments including "Thou shall not steal" instilled within him a sense of righteousness. Like an artisan shaping a pot out of clay, Christianity molded Randolph's character and helped to define his future as a trailblazer who worked to dismantle the pillars of institutional racism.

Beyond the word of God giving inspiration to African-Americans, the role of the church within the lives of African-Americans was instrumental in helping them survive. The racist taunts African-Americans endured when they walked to work, the dirty washrooms they were forced to use, and the fear of getting lynched just for staring at a White woman, created psychological trauma within the community. One false move, one accident, one innocent mistake could bring your life to a tragic end. African-Americans were mindful they were vulnerable to malicious attacks by White people. And White people knew African-Americans were easy, low-hanging fruit they could exploit, abuse and, if need be, kill if they so desired. History was littered with examples of African-Americans who were killed as a result of overzealous, mean-spirited racist White people. The fear African-Americans had towards Whites was justified because it was grounded in reality. African-Americans realized they were under attack, but there was nowhere to hide. No place to celebrate their unique culture and history without being vilified. No space to reaffirm their bonds within their community.

This void was filled by the church. Behind the stained-glass windows and the walls which were made of cedar, pine wood and bricks was a community which formed an African-American metropolis, a Wakanda which celebrated its cultural distinctiveness. Not only did the church protect African-Americans psychologically, but it also became a source of strength. The church was a powerful adhesive which kept the African-American community together. It served as a space for African-Americans to network, pool resources, exchange ideas and to combat racism.[61] After a long sermon by the preacher, families would gather in the church basement, participate in fellowship and feast on foods like macaroni and cheese, collard greens, fried chicken, orca and fried green tomatoes. Children would play hopscotch, tag and hide-and-go seek. Friendships were forged. Bonds were cemented. African-Americans could celebrate their culture in safety outside of the judgmental, condescending gaze of White America. Randolph's religious faith, sustained and nurtured within the African Methodist Episcopal (AME) church, informed his political

---

[61] Cornelius L. Bynum, *A. Philip Randolph and the Struggle for Civil Rights* (Chicago: University of Illinois Press, 2010), 24.

stance on racism. For Randolph, religion and racism were like Siamese twins, two sides of the same coin.[62] Following the tenets of Christianity meant resisting White supremacy. So, the African-American church became the driving force behind the political struggle for equality for African-Americans.[63]

Just as important as Randolph's racial consciousness, his devotion to socialism also was a driving force behind his civic activism. His class-consciousness, developed while he was a student at City College of New York (CCNY), encouraged him to embrace elements of socialism. College afforded Randolph with an opportunity to learn about socialist concepts like how the production and distribution of wealth should be regulated by the entire community.[64] He also witnessed his classmates organize in support of workers' rights.[65] When Randolph left CCNY in 1914, his outlook on life had changed from viewing the international community strictly through a racial lens to a worldview which included class.[66] Most importantly, he was now ready to put his ideas into action. His arrest for his participation at an antiwar rally in Cleveland, Ohio in 1917 signaled a shift in his behavior. Randolph's identity was now informing his behavior. He was acting upon his beliefs, in spite of the inherent dangers of being an African-American male committed to destroying institutional racism.

---

[62]   Bynum, *A. Philip Randolph and the Struggle for Civil Rights*, 27.
[63]   Ibid.
[64]   Ibid., 67.
[65]   Ibid.
[66]   Ibid.

Randolph's embrace of socialism was anchored by his desire to end racism. Socialists sought to empower workers by ending their exploitation by the business community. Since African-Americans were the most exploited group, socialists had an obligation to fight for their rights. Like the old saying, "The enemy of my enemy is my friend" the abuse African-Americans experienced in the work force made them a natural ally to the Socialist movement. Randolph viewed the Socialist Party as the best way for African-Americans to advocate for their rights.[67] Labor parity meant racial equality. In his eyes, the biggest problem facing African-Americans was they were unable to sell their labor within the marketplace in a way that maximized their earning potential.[68] His solution was simple. African-Americans had to unionize.[69] Industrial capitalism had to be reimagined.[70] And the Socialist Party had to emerge as a legitimate political entity.[71] If these issues were addressed, Randolph believed the state of the African-American community would improve.

Randolph put his socialist views into action through his efforts to form the Brotherhood of Sleeping Car Porters. His contribution to unionizing African-American Pullman Porters was one of his greatest achievements as a civil rights leader. It provided a blueprint on how the African-American community could leverage its political weight to make meaningful change. The victory Randolph helped secure for the Pullman

---

[67]   Ibid., 69.

[68]   Ibid.

[69]   Ibid.

[70]   Ibid.

[71]   Ibid.

Porters would inspire African-Americans thirty years later as they fought to secure the right to vote.

The Pullman Palace Car Company, founded in 1867 by George Pullman, became the gold standard for luxury travel in the 1920s and 1930s. Pullman was at once an extraordinary entrepreneur, a tyrant and a social activist. Pullman was born on March 3rd, 1831 to James and Emily Pullman. Short and a little pudgy, his unassuming demeanor made people easily write him off as a fourth grade dropout who would not amount to much in life, a boy who would turn into a man and live off the fruits of his father's labor. Pullman would prove the doubters wrong. After his father died, Pullman took over his father's business of moving large buildings. When he moved to Chicago, he successfully secured a contract to move buildings as high as ten feet above ground and onto new foundations to accommodate for a new sewer system which was recently installed.[72]

Pullman's brainchild to build a better sleeper was a reflection of his creativity and his ability to locate a niche he could exploit within the railroad industry. After traveling from work on a railway sleeper, he realized the experience was intolerable because he did not get a good night's rest. When his train reached its destination, he was tired and stressed because the sleeper lacked poor ventilation, felt cramped and stuffy, was loud and shook constantly. In his mind, the sleeper car needed an upgrade. Pullman set out to build a better sleeping car and he did. The newly designed

---

[72]   "George Pullman: Pullman Sleeper Railroad Car," LEMELSON – MIT, accessed November 24th, 2020, https://lemelson.mit.edu/resources/george-pullman.

Pullman cars were so gorgeous eventually they became the preferred way of travel for hundreds of thousands of Americans. Roughly one hundred thousand people every night would tuck themselves into bed in one of the several thousand opulent Pullman cars crisscrossing the country.[73] Expensive dark walnut wood paneling lined its interior. Plush carpet, thick silk shades, brass chandeliers and beautiful stained-glass windows adorned each Pullman car. Pullman cars were wider and taller than traditional sleepers, making the passenger experience on them more comfortable. They were outfitted with rubberized springs to minimize bouncing and shaking.[74] Pullman sleeping cars were like Waldorf Astoria suites on wheels.

Pullman cars were famous not only for their aesthetic beauty, but also for the porters who provided excellent service. After the Civil War ended, Pullman hired many former slaves from the South to work as porters. He reasoned former slaves would make the perfect servants on the train. They worked long shifts (sometimes for twenty-one hours at a time) for extremely low wages and would carry out their duties without question. Skin color even factored into Pullman's vision of the perfect experience on his Pullman cars. He believed darker-skinned African-American

---

[73] Dean Reynolds, "Pullman railcars: A detour back through time" YouTube Video, April 13th, 2014, CBS Morning News, 5:18, https://www.youtube.com/watch?v=PhZw1tKgxkc.

[74] Jimmy Stamp, "Traveling in Style and Comfort: The Pullman Sleeping Car," *Smithsonian Magazine,* December 11th, 2013, https://www.smithsonianmag.com/arts-culture/traveling-style-and-comfort-pullman-sleeping-car-180949300/.

Pullman Porters would put middle-class and upper-middle-class White passengers at ease because it would make them feel more comfortable.[75]

Once hired, Pullman Porters went through a rigorous training regimen. They learned how to take down and put up beds efficiently. They were taught how to clean sleeping areas. They became experts at shining shoes. They were instructed on how to properly carry luggage onto a train. And they learned how to deal with racism from passengers. Sometimes passengers would call a Pullman Car Porter "George," after George Pullman, or "Boy," a derogatory name for African-American men. Sometimes passengers would tell racially charged jokes, often in front of African-American Pullman Porters. The porters would grin and ignore the comments, fearing if they spoke up they would lose their jobs. Frank Rollins, a former Pullman Porter, said his trainer at the Pullman Company once told him, "Look you are going to run into some indignities. And you do not have to accept them. Whenever any passenger makes you unhappy about anything, you can just speak your mind but you wait until you get back to the men's room by yourself."[76] Pullman Porters learned how to manage their anger. Their livelihoods depended on it.

Pullman Porters would, however, fight back by organizing the first African-American union. Ashley Totten, a Pullman Porter and editor of the *Messenger* (a literary and political magazine by and for African-Amer-

---

[75]   "Pullman Porters," *History*, October 8th, 2021, https://www.history.com/topics/black-history/pullman-porters.

[76]   *All Things Considered*, "Former Pullman Porter Subtly Confronted Racism," presented by Michele Norris and Robert Siegel, aired May 8th, 2009, on NPR. https://www.npr.org/templates/story/story.php?storyId=103945861.

icans), was looking for a way to secure more rights for African-American Pullman Porters. Medium build with a semi-dark mocha complexion and an easy, laid-back demeanor, Totten became one of the founders of the Brotherhood of Sleeping Car Porters. Yet, he needed help. So, Totten, along with a few other Pullman Porters, approached Asa Randolph in New York's Central Park station and asked him if he would lead a union comprised of African-American Pullman Porters.[77] After thinking it over, Randolph accepted the offer.

Deciding to lead a movement to create a union for the Pullman Porters came with risks. Beneath the veneer of the Pullman Company as a respectable, socially conscious business was a ruthless, vindicative organization which operated more like a crime syndicate than a legitimate enterprise. The Pullman Company would stop at nothing to win. If they had to lie, cheat, steal or intimidate to accomplish their goals, they would do it. From the Pullman Company's perspective, Randolph and others who were seeking to create an independent African-American union were ungrateful troublemakers who needed to be taught a lesson.

The Pullman Company used a number of methods, including spying, to inform on African-American men who were seeking to organize an all-Black union.[78] Disguising themselves as fellow workers, moles would befriend real Pullman Porters and get them to disclose their feelings and thoughts about the Pullman Company. Informers working on behalf of

---

[77]   Jervis Anderson, *A. Philip Randolph – A Biographical Portrait* (Berkeley: University of California Press, 1972), 168.

[78]   Anderson, *A. Philip Randolph – A Biographical Portrait*, 178.

the Pullman Company would also provide intelligence on the tactics and strategies devised by Randolph and other leaders in the union.[79] Like the usage of radar during the Battle of Britain which gave the British Royal Air Force time to track German warplanes and to get airborne so as to engage with them before they attacked cities like London and Liverpool, the Pullman Company's network of spies gave them a clear advantage against Randolph. The Pullman Company knew what Randolph and the union were going to do before they did it. This gave the company time to make moves which would nullify plans Randolph sought to implement.

Violence was another weapon the Pullman Company used in its war against Randolph. The threat of violence was a simple, easy way to get some African-Americans to bend to the will of the company. The Pullman Company used brutality to send a message to African-Americans seeking to organize their own all-Black union — stop organizing or else. The Pullman Company funded a small army of local toughs who beat the living daylights out of some African-American Pullman Porters seeking to join the Brotherhood of Sleeping Car Porters. A busted lip, broken nose and a few fractured ribs were all that was required to discourage some African-Americans from joining the union.[80] Ashley Totten felt the wrath of the Pullman Company after he was clubbed nearly to death by some local thugs. The bruises, black eye, broken bones and lacerations from the beating was a painful reminder to him and others that the Pullman

---

[79]   Ibid.
[80]   Ibid.

Company would stop at nothing to destroy the Brotherhood of Sleeping Car Porters.

The battle over the hearts and minds of African-Americans and their perception of the Pullman Company and the Brotherhood of Sleeping Car Porters was arguably the most important factor in whether or not the union would succeed. In this game of public perception, nothing was off limits. The Pullman Company had a ton of money which bought them influence within the African-American press. With journalists, columnists, photographers, editors and publicists on their payroll, the Pullman Company sought to shape how the African-American community perceived the Brotherhood of Sleeping Car Porters. Pundits wrote articles which portrayed the African-American union in a negative light. African-American newspapers ran stories which were either fabricated or gross distortions of the truth. Big, bold headlines like "Asa Randolph works to destroy the relationship African-Americans have with the Pullman Company" were commonly found in newspapers like the *Defender*. And "Big Negroes" with social and political capital were hired to attack the reputation of Randolph and the overall mission of the Brotherhood of Sleeping Car Porters.[81] Influential African-American business leaders and politicians gave speeches denouncing Randolph's efforts to create the union. Simply put, the Pullman Company developed a comprehensive battlefield strategy to discredit and, ultimately, destroy Randolph's plan to unionize African-American Pullman Porters.

---

[81] Ibid.

The Pullman Company even sought to manipulate how African-Americans viewed the Brotherhood of Sleeping Car Porters through the church. Spiritual leaders of the church were respected figures within the African-American community, idolized by many as living representatives of God. Through these trusted religious leaders, African-Americans were given psychological armor which helped them cope with the unrelenting onslaught of racism they frequently experienced. Given their stature in the African-American community, the Pullman Company made the decision to put African-American religious leaders on their payrolls. With help from religious leaders, the Pullman Company's disdain for Randolph and the Brotherhood of Sleeping Car Porters was now wrapped in the vernacular of Christianity.

Access to the sacred space of the church enabled the Pullman Company to seize the moral high ground in their battle with Randolph. African-American congregations were now trained to view the confrontation between the Pullman Company and the Brotherhood of Sleeping Car Porters through a religious lens. Reverends unleashed their venom in the pulpit by giving passionate sermons ridiculing the groundbreaking union as evil. They demonized Randolph, claiming he was morally bankrupt. These religious leaders were shielded from criticism.[82] If the preacher said the Brotherhood of Sleeping Car Porters was working on behalf of the devil, then it must be true. Therefore, the vitriolic message

---

[82]   Ibid.

18

religious leaders shouted from their pulpits was not scrutinized but taken at face value.

It was like a game of poker where the Pullman Company appeared to have a set of diamonds ace, king, queen, joker and 10 (aka a royal flush) and Randolph had a collection of two 8 of clubs, one 2 of spades and two 7 of spades. They played to win. The battle to unionize the Pullman Company seemed like a losing cause. The Pullman Company manipulated African-Americans perception of the Brotherhood of Sleeping Car Porters in both secular and sacred spaces. If violence or manipulation did not work at discouraging African-Americans from joining the union, the Pullman Company suspended or, in a worse-case scenarios, fired African-American Pullman Porters. It was not a fair scrimmage. Randolph showed up to a fight with the Pullman Company with the wrong weapon. He brought a switchblade when in reality he needed a gun.

Nevertheless, Randolph remained committed to his cause of creating a union for the Pullman Porters. He felt he had an obligation to help them, especially since he gave them hope they would eventually get a union which would represent their interests.[83] As Randolph's cause suffered defeat after defeat, his physical appearance deteriorated. His shoes had no soles. His clothes became raggedy and began to fray.[84] He looked like a man one paycheck away from being put out on the street. Yet, this could not be further from the truth. Beneath this rough and tired exterior, his

---

[83]   Ibid., 193.
[84]   Ibid., 214.

determination to fight on was never stronger. By concentrating more on his devotion to his cause and less on his outward appearance, Randolph's substance of character came to light. He wanted to be evaluated on what he accomplished for the African-American community, not on how well his clothes looked or fit on him.

Ultimately, Randolph would eventually prevail. During the Roosevelt Administration, the National Industry Recovery Bill was passed which protected employees' right to organize and to bargain collectively through representatives which they decided on. Most importantly, the bill explicitly stated companies like the Pullman Company could not intimidate their employees.[85] Seizing the moment, Randolph sent a proposal to the Pullman Company which guaranteed Pullman Porters better working conditions. Randolph's proposition demanded the porters work only two hundred and forty hours a month, not four hundred hours every four weeks.[86] The Pullman Company reluctantly agreed to Randolph's proposal. Despite suffering numerous setbacks, he prevailed in getting the Pullman Company to acknowledge not only the Brotherhood of Sleeping Car Porters, but also in accepting terms which enhanced their working conditions. Consequently, the Pullman Company took one step closer to shedding the perception that African-American Pullman Porters were glorified slaves who were helping to reconstruct the comforts afforded to Whites during the Antebellum Period in the South.

---

[85]   Ibid., 217.

[86]   Ibid., 225.

Randolph's rising political status coincided with the influx of African-Americans migrating north. In what became known as the Great Migration, African-American men and women left the South for better paying jobs and to escape the constant threat of racial violence they experienced.[87] They were tired of being humiliated. They were exhausted from dealing with the prospect that one misinterpreted look or one misunderstood comment they gave or made to a White person could get them killed. They were tired of being tired. In the eyes of many African-Americans, the North became an idealized wonderland of milk and honey where they could be themselves. A land which was free from fear and from the suffocating way of life afforded to them in the South. The South had put a hunch in the backs of millions of African-Americans. The excessive curvature in their backs was symbolic. It meant their prospects in life were dim and bleak. Many African-Americans believed the North could straighten out this curve in their spines, helping them to walk a little taller and with a little more dignity. The North could give them hope by injecting new meaning into their lives through access to better paying jobs. In effect, African-Americans could take their gaze which was directed at the ground and look life right in the eyes, smile and say, "Is that all you got?"

The migration of African-Americans to cities like Chicago, Philadelphia and New York came at a cost though. As African-Americans poured into northern metropolises, they were not greeted with open arms.

---

[87]   Paula Pfeffer, *A. Philip Randolph, Pioneer of the Civil Rights Movement* (Baton Rouge: Louisiana State University Press, 1990), 45.

White folks did not knock on the doors of African-Americans who had recently arrived from the South and hand them freshly baked apple pies, delicious honey baked hams with a pitcher of iced tea. They did not give African-Americans big hugs and plant wet kisses on their foreheads and cheeks. Nope. White people largely viewed them with skepticism and even hostility. To many White Americans, African-Americans were foreign invaders akin to leeches who would suck the life, vitality and innate goodness out of these urban centers and infuse them with criminality, sexually transmitted diseases and rampant violence.

Beyond these incredibly racist and demeaning stereotypes which many Whites harbored towards African-Americans, the perceived threat of losing their jobs to African-Americans created anxiety for many of them. Contention over jobs exacerbated racial tensions between Whites and African-Americans.[88] Like pouring lighter fluid on a fire, heightened competition for jobs ignited resentment within the White community. Whites were accustomed to job security. For many, the whiteness of their skin guaranteed they would get and keep a job. They could rob a bank and set a house on fire and, when they got out of prison, their job would be waiting for them. The prospect of losing their jobs, especially to African-Americans, was horrifying. Some believed losing jobs to African-Americans amounted to a decline in their social status and diminished their economic power. Some even embraced an illogical form of White victimization, with some Whites believing African-Americans

---

[88] Pfeffer, *A. Philip Randolph, Pioneer of the Civil Rights Movement*, 45.

who were securing employment were doing so at their expense. In their eyes, African-Americans were taking jobs which *should* have gone to qualified Whites.

White victimization inverted the oppressor/oppressed model which neatly summarized the power dynamic between Whites and African-Americans. In this *Stranger Things* Upside Down World logic, an alternate dimension was imagined. Whites were forced to ride in the back of buses, provided inferior health care and forced to send their children to overcrowded schools with few resources. Whites, not African-Americans, were being persecuted as a result of the color of their skin. As a consequence of these sentiments, some Whites residing in working class communities in big metropolitan cities throughout the North did harbor bitterness towards African-Americans.

Meanwhile, African-Americans welcomed the dismantling of the unequal power structure between African-Americans and Whites. It meant more wealth would be equally distributed between African-Americans and Whites. African-Americans could provide for their families. They too could strive for the American dream. Unfortunately, their goal of securing the American dream was a figment of their imagination; cotton candy that looked good and initially tasted wonderful until it quickly melted in their mouths. Since African-Americans were not in a position of power, they knew their options were limited and they would not be given a fair shot to secure jobs in the labor market.[89] African-Americans

---

[89]   Ibid.

were firmly situated at the bottom of the socio-economic ladder. Understandably, they were livid.

Randolph understood this anger had to be channeled in a productive manner, so he organized an equality movement which focused on desegregating the U.S. military.[90] The integration of African-Americans into the U.S. military was considered by some to be a key victory in the civil rights movement. As defenders of the country, soldiers in the U.S. military had a prominent role in American society, particularly during the 1930s and 1940s. As a result, many soldiers were revered. Some African-Americans believed the social and political capital garnered by African-American men fighting for their country would shatter stereotypes that they were cowards, morally bankrupt, irresponsible and not intelligent. Others thought it would prove beyond a shadow of a doubt that African-American men were *men*. It would signal to White America that African-American men were just as smart and committed to preserving their democracy as they were. Some even surmised it would force White America to accept African-Americans as their equal.

The psychological benefits of being a part of the U.S. military were numerous. African-American soldiers who wore the U.S. military uniform were associated with power and prestige, terms which usually were not used to describe them. Wearing the uniform signaled to others they were warriors, protectors of America and its values. When they entered a room, people took note. Men wearing a U.S. military uniform were

---

[90]   Ibid.

sending a message — they *meant* business. These were men of substance and purpose. They put loyalty, bravery and honor above life itself. And, consequently, they earned the right to stick their chest out with pride, to walk with their heads held high and their backs straight. And it implied they now too were Americans.

African-American men got enjoyment out of not only wearing the uniform, but also its effect on White Americans. African-American men wearing U.S. military uniforms boggled their minds and shook their reality. Wearing a U.S. military uniform meant if African-American men were willing and able to die for their country it demonstrated they did not fit into the box labeled "Boy" which America had placed them in. It indicated they exhibited qualities such as responsibility, discipline and commitment to a cause. All attributes typically ascribed to men, not boys. If these men were willing to put their lives on the line to protect democracy, they deserved all of the fruits American democracy had to offer. They deserved to send their children to whatever school they wanted them to go to and to have access to the best health care. It suggested they had a right to move into any community they chose. And, it insinuated that African-American soldiers had a right to serve in a military which valued them just as much as it treasured White soldiers.

Randolph believed ending Jim Crow in the U.S. Armed Forces would ignite a tidal wave of social change, which ultimately could bring an end to institutional racism.[91] His efforts to desegregate the U.S. military were

---

[91]   Ibid., 133.

revolutionary at the time. African-Americans typically did not *demand* change. They *begged* for change. The institution of slavery and its successor, sharecropping, coupled with the emergence of Jim Crow laws which legalized racial segregation, conditioned many African-Americans not to speak up for themselves and to accept the status quo. Many did a cost/benefit analysis before taking on racism in America. Most African-Americans deduced it was just not worth losing their job, their home or their life if their calls for equality and respect angered White Americans. The fear of White retribution encouraged many African-Americans to remain quiet, even if deep down inside they wanted to fight back.

Randolph was, however, special. He would not take no for an answer. Like Harry Houdini's mind-blowing escape from a water tank while in a straitjacket with his feet securely locked, Randolph found a way to get the U.S. military to desegregate, at least on paper. Even so, he would face an uphill battle against the U.S. military. The African-American community did have some economic power, though it was not powerful enough to make the American political establishment force the U.S. military to end segregation. Some African-Americans owned and operated businesses such as car washes, jewelry shops and boutique clothing stores in cities across America in the 1940s. Policy Kings, who controlled large, sophisticated gambling rackets in places such as New York, Chicago and Detroit, made millions of dollars and generated thousands of jobs for African-Americans. Despite this fact, the economic might of the African-American community paled in comparison to the larger White community. Most importantly, the community's financial system operated exclusively within the confines of its own borders, and was not directly connected to White financial institutions where the real money in the American economy resided. Consequently, African-Americans did not have the huge capital necessary to make large donations to influential politicians who could cajole the U.S. military into giving up its policy of "separate but equal" within the U.S. Armed Forces.

Randolph also realized the African-American community's social capital was minimal. A White male partner at a law firm might have a friendly conversation with an African-American janitor in the lobby or a White stay-at-home mom might have coffee in her kitchen with her African-American cleaning lady, but that was about it. Real, authentic relationships between African-Americans and Whites were rare, especially in the 1940s. Most Whites did not and would not associate with African-Americans. They considered them beneath themselves, little more than tools which served to enhance their own lives. Likewise, many African-Americans harbored a mixture of respect, fear and resentment towards White people. Because African-Americans functioned within a system controlled by Whites, they knew their fate was often determined by whether or not White people liked and/or felt comfortable around them.

Beyond the racial norms of the 1940s, Jim Crow laws ensured African-Americans and Whites lived separate lives. They worshiped in separate churches. They ate in separate restaurants. They lived in separate communities. Like an invisible twenty-foot wall erected between Whites and African-Americans, Jim Crow laws guaranteed real bonds could not and would not be established between African-Americans and Whites. And, if White America could not see how racism had an impact on African-Americans, then it meant they could not fully empathize with African-Americans and their struggle for equality. In other words, Jim Crow laws prohibited some White Americans from seeing and feeling the oppression African-Americans were subjected to on a daily basis in America.

Literature, however, did provide a window into the lives of African-Americans which White America could look through and observe their suffering. Literature had been a weapon in the arsenal against the fight against slavery and racial injustice. Books like *Uncle Tom's Cabin* by Harriett Beecher Stowe, which made a powerful case against the institution of slavery, did spark a wave of anti-slavery sentiment which prompted the North to go to war with the South. More recently, books like Richard Wright's *Black Boy* and *Native Son* cracked open the door for White America to see the emotional pain and racial trauma African-Americans faced. These books afforded White Americans a chance to sip from the chalice of pain, sorrow and misery which African-Americans had been drinking from since their ancestors set foot in America hundreds of years earlier as slaves.

Yet, the poignant messages on race embedded in Wright's books was not enough to spark a social or racial awakening. The racial consciousness these two books provided to White America was buried beneath thousands of other books written about a range of other topics in the 1940s. As a result, the racial intelligence and emotional awareness of White people on race matters in the 1940s was abysmal. Many White people just did not get it, and this was by design. White people did not understand the struggle for equality because they never really got to know African-Americans beyond the superficial encounters they had with them at work. The few White people who did empathize with the African-American experience were not equipped with either the requisite courage or the political/social power to actually create meaningful change for millions of African-Americans.

If African-Americans wanted racial progress to take hold in America, they had to push the agenda. The only real, tangible power the community had was in its numbers. As the largest minority group in the United States in the late 1940s, the African-American community was a sleeping giant. The sheer number of African-Americans living in cities like Chicago, New York and Washington D.C. indicated the community was a formidable force. Randolph understood this fact and devised a plan which would leverage the large numbers of African-Americans in America to his advantage in his fight to desegregate the U.S. military. To achieve this goal, Randolph tapped into the subconsciousness of White America where racism lingered. The racism Whites harbored towards African-Americans overtime translated into animosity and, most importantly, fear. Some Whites believed African-Americans would exact revenge on them for their persecution and torture as slaves. White men feared African-American men would rape their women, even though the inverse of this happened in history as large scale rape of African-American women by White men took place for decades on plantations throughout the South.

Understandably, the mental and physical cruelty African-Americans experienced as a result of slavery made most of them incredibly angry towards White people. The beatings, constant humiliation and psychological torture African-Americans were frequently subjected to had taken its toll on them. This apprehension towards White America was a natural response to the living hell they existed in during slavery and beyond. Many White people realized even though slavery had technically ended, African-Americans were still treated poorly. Some White people suspected African-Americans wanted to even the score with their oppressor. They wanted revenge. They believed it was not a question of if but when would African-Americans strike back at White America, leaving bloody bodies and burning buildings in their wake.

Randolph understood White fear of the African-American community. And he knew he could use this fear to bend the American political establishment to his will. If fear could be used to mobilize White people for evil like lynching an African-American man for breaking an *unspoken* rule, it could also be used for good, like desegregating the U.S. military. He surmised the marshalling of hundreds of thousands of African-Americans onto the streets of Washington D.C. would scare the living daylights out of White people.[92] White people's worst fears of African-Americans would come to the surface and become a reality. In their minds, bank robberies would skyrocket. Wholesale raping of White women by sexually deviant African-American men would take place. Sexually transmitted diseases would be as common as catching a cold. Violence would spread throughout the greater Washington D.C. area like an uncontrollable wildfire. America's beloved capital would no longer be the shining city on a hill which epitomized the very best values and beliefs of a free and open democratic society. Instead, it would be a city akin to Sodom and Gomorrah. A devil's paradise.

Further, Randolph concluded White people would rather leave Washington D.C. than witness African-Americans tear down their city. White women would run for their lives and White men would pick up their shotguns and shoot at any African-American who came within a hundred yards of their homes. An exodus of White people fleeing Washington D.C. would take place. White people would grab their belongings, pack up a few sandwiches, snatch their babies, throw a few articles of clothing into a bag and run for their lives. Businesses would feel the effects of Whites leaving and go bankrupt, hurting the local economy. Schools would close. Hospitals would shut down. Washington D.C. would

---

[92]   Ibid., 48.

become a shell of itself; a once prosperous city would now be a desolate, bleak metropolis drained of the immense political energy it once generated as the capital of the most powerful country in the world. President Roosevelt's worst nightmare which kept him up at night would become a reality. Randolph was certain Roosevelt would do everything in his power to avoid this scenario.[93]

Randolph's plan was simple — organize a massive march in Washington in protest of African-Americans being locked out of jobs generated by World War II and being excluded from New Deal programs.[94] First, he created the March on Washington organization. The formation of the March on Washington group was Randolph's warning shot to Roosevelt over jobs which African-Americans were excluded from during World War II and from New Deal programs they were barred from getting. Through his vast network of informants and political operatives, President Roosevelt learned about the upcoming march and wanted to prevent it from taking place. President Roosevelt had to address the ensuing political thunderstorm gathering on the horizon. So, President Roosevelt made the first move. He summoned Randolph to the White House to discuss his demands.

President Roosevelt was a towering political figure. The 32nd President of the United States was born on January 30th, 1882 in Hyde Park, New York to James and Sara Roosevelt, a distant cousin to Teddy Roos-

---

[93]   Ibid., 45.

[94]   "March on Washington," *History*, accessed October 29, 2009, https://www.history.com/topics/black-history/march-on-washington.

evelt, the 26th President of the United States. Having made their money in real estate, the Roosevelt family was part of the American aristocracy. Roosevelt traveled throughout the United States and Europe with his father, which helped to deepen and broaden his perspective of the world.[95] Roosevelt was provided excellent tutors and governesses which injected into him a natural curiosity for the world around him.

At fourteen, Roosevelt was sent off to Groton, a prestigious private college-preparatory school in New England. The move from the safe confines of his parents' estate in Hyde Park, New York, where he was the center of attention, to Groton meant Roosevelt was no longer the puppet master who reigned supreme over his environment. He was forced to break out of his mold, make new friends and build new alliances with others. Roosevelt would meet and eventually exceed this social challenge Groton presented to him when he was a young adolescent. By his senior year, he would distinguish himself as a competent student, a solid athlete and traces of his formidable leadership skills were slowly beginning to emerge as a dormitory prefect.[96]

At Harvard, Roosevelt further sharpened his interpersonal skills through his active participation in a wide range of clubs. He joined the Fly Club, the Hasty Pudding, the Institute of 1770, the Dickey, the Signet Society, the Yacht Club, the Glee Club, the Memorial Society and the St.

---

[95]   "Childhood of FDR," *History Central*, accessed Wednesday, December 28th, 2020, https://www. historycentral.com/FDR/FDRchild.html.

[96]   Ibid.

Paul's Society and many more.[97] In most of these clubs, Roosevelt took on leadership responsibilities which helped him fine-tune his problem-solving skills, develop his ability to collaborate with others, and learn when and how to compromise for the greater good of the organization.

Additionally, Roosevelt's personality was beginning to take shape. He now was more upbeat, charming and gregarious. He still harbored a New Englander's reserve and aloofness, but also had an accessibility which made it easy for others to work with him and to seek him out for guidance and direction. His magnetic personality and his big, juicy, warm smile made Roosevelt hard to dislike. Winston Churchill, the famous British statesman who served as Prime Minster of Great Britain during World War II, recalled meeting President Roosevelt for the first time akin to "opening his first bottle of champagne."[98] Coupled with his stunning personality, Roosevelt's organizational and managerial skills which were cultivated in college helped him climb the American political establishment, first as a state senator from New York, then as an Assistant Secretary of the Navy, then Governor of New York and finally as the 32nd President of the United States.

President Roosevelt's negotiation skills would be put to the test as he engaged with Randolph on African-Americans access to jobs during

---

[97] Philip M. Boffey "Franklin Delano Roosevelt at Harvard," *The Harvard Crimson*, December 13th, 2020, https://www.thecrimson.com/article/1957/12/13/franklin-delano-roosevelt-at-harvard-phis-torians/.

[98] Ron Elving, "'Franklin D. Roosevelt: A Political Life' Examines The Personal Traits That Marked FDR For Greatness," review of *Franklin D. Roosevelt: A Political Life* by Robert Dallek, *NPR online Book Review*, November 8, 2017, https://www.npr.org/2017/11/08/562251084/franklin-d-roosevelt-a-political-life-examines-the-personal-traits-that-marked-f.

World War II. In 1941, millions of jobs were created as America was preparing to go to war against Nazi Germany and Imperial Japan. Many of these new jobs were in urban centers. Seeking an opportunity to be gainfully employed, African-Americans applied for these jobs. Even so, African-Americans who attempted to take advantage of these employment opportunities were met with violence and discrimination. In many cases, they were rejected for these new jobs because of their skin color.

When Randolph was called by President Roosevelt to the White House to discuss the march in Washington, he assumed he would have his hands full. Randolph knew President Roosevelt was a legend, a political rock star of sorts. Randolph was aware of the immense power President Roosevelt wielded not only in the United States, but throughout the world. He was cognizant of President Roosevelt's savvy, smooth, dripping in charm style of politics. He understood President Roosevelt had deep connections within the business community. Randolph was aware of President Roosevelt's influence within the political establishment of the United States. Because of these things, Randolph recognized President Roosevelt usually got what he wanted.

President Roosevelt, on the other hand, thought Randolph was out of his league. He presumed Randolph was a political novice who thought more highly of himself than he actually was. He believed Randolph could easily be bent to his will. The President assumed Randolph's skin color, dearth of intellect and courage, lack of coming from the right type of family with the right type of connections and the mediocre schools he attended, indicated he was a political lightweight who was beneath him. Most importantly, Roosevelt believed Randolph desperately needed to be put in his place.

So, when President Roosevelt looked Randolph in the eye and ordered him to stop organizing a march in Washington, he was signaling to him to shut up, sit down and back off attempting to broaden the accessibility of New Deal programs to the African-American community. In President Roosevelt's mind, this was what African-Americans like Randolph were *supposed* to do when powerful White men gave directives. They took orders and followed them. When Randolph said "No," Roosevelt was left speechless. His assumptions shattered into a million little pieces. He underestimated Randolph. In that moment, the President realized his status, power and privilege meant nothing to the revered social activist. The racial prism President Roosevelt viewed and interpreted Randolph thru skewed his vision of the civil rights leader. The President thought Randolph was a political novice who would soon capitulate to his demands. President Roosevelt was wrong. Randolph was in his own right an astute political mastermind who possessed formidable negotiation skills. In truth, Randolph was President Roosevelt's equal.

Randolph stood firm. He refused to call the protest off until real concessions were put on the table which would help to end desegregation in the U.S. military.[99] Once President Roosevelt observed Randolph could not be bullied, he resorted to looking for other ways to solve the problem. He went into crisis mode. His objective was to prevent a political catastrophe at all costs. So, he wisely compromised. As a result of the threat of a massive march in Washington, President Roosevelt signed Executive Order No. 8802, which led to the creation of the Fair Employment Practices Committee.[100]

The civil rights activist outmaneuvered President Roosevelt through his usage of political jujitsu. By threatening him with the prospect of a march in Washington, he knew he was tapping into racial fear embedded in President Roosevelt's subconscious mind. Evoking these fears in President Roosevelt's mind threw him off balance. President Roosevelt assumed the aftermath of a massive demonstration of African-Americans marching in Washington would be akin to setting off a political bomb within the capital of the United States. Political fatalities from the explosion would be almost unimaginable. In his mind, he had no choice but to reach an agreement with Randolph.

Despite this victory, Randolph acknowledged the goal of desegregating the U.S. military was still but a dream. African-Americans continued to face discrimination. In the mid to late 1940s, African-Americans were still accepted into the U.S. military on a limited basis. Once they got into the U.S. military, they were immediately subjected to Jim Crow

---

[99] Paula Pfeffer, *A. Philip Randolph, Pioneer of the Civil Rights Movement* (Baton Rouge: Louisiana State University Press, 1990), 49.

[100] Pfeffer, *A. Philip Randolph, Pioneer of the Civil Rights Movement*, 49.

laws.[101] African-Americans rode in separate train cars. They lived in segregated barracks. They shopped at separate stores and went to segregated theaters.[102] The U.S. military was essentially two armies: one African-American and one White. To unify the U.S. military, Randolph knew more planning and organizing had to be done.

So, after World War II, he developed a strategy which aimed to bring an end to racial inequity within the U.S. military. Randolph waged war on desegregating the U.S. military in two ways. First, he attacked the concept of Jim Crow within U.S. military law. Second, he would again rely on African-Americans, in this case youth, to take on desegregating the U.S. military by advocating for themselves.[103] The second movement, the League for Non-Violent Civil Disobedience Against Military Segregation, focused on the youth. The organization encouraged African-American youth to stand up and fight against segregation within military establishments.[104] These two movements, together, put pressure on President Truman and his administration to address racial discrimination against African-Americans in the U.S. Armed Forces.

After President Roosevelt died in 1944, his vice president, Harry Truman, became the 33rd President of the United States. President Truman was the exact opposite of President Roosevelt. Truman did not come from a wealthy, well connected New England family; he was not born on

---

[101]   Ibid., 134.
[102]   Ibid.
[103]   Ibid., 133 – 134.
[104]   Ibid.

a massive estate in Hyde Park, New York. Unlike Roosevelt, Truman was not provided with tutors and governesses who created individualized curricula which helped to maximize his intellectual capacities, deepening and widening his thought process while also stoking the flames of intellectual curiosity. He did not have a magnetic personality who people tended to gravitate towards. He did not have movie star good looks. He did not have extraordinary communication skills which were used to win political debates. His bland personality foretold Truman's future prospects in life. He was destined to have an ordinary, uneventful existence on the planet. Ironically, Truman would defy the odds, shatter expectations and chart his own course to greatness.

Truman was born on May 8th, 1884 in Lamar, Missouri. His parents, John and Martha Truman, were industrious, hardworking people from the Midwest. Truman's father, the breadwinner of the household, was a farmer and livestock dealer. He bought and sold cattle, sheep, horses, pigs and goats. He also harvested crops and sold them on the open market. Meanwhile, Martha oversaw the domestic sphere of the Truman household. She stayed at home cooking, cleaning and taking care of Truman and his two other siblings, John and Mary Jane.

Truman initially lived in Independence, Missouri with his father. When his father's livestock business went under, he moved to Kansas City, Missouri to look for a job.[105] After struggling to find work, Truman moved to his grandfather's farm where he worked and lived for roughly

---

[105]   Ibid., 1.

a decade.[106] Truman's experience living on his grandfather's farm was transformative. During this time, he developed his confidence and he became more outgoing and affable.[107] He could carry a conversation and put people at ease. He further honed his interpersonal skills by joining the Freemasons, the largest fraternal organization in the world. More importantly, Truman joined the local Democratic Party, which foreshadowed the beginning of his distinguished political career.[108] And, Truman signed up for and served in the U.S. military where he was in the National Guard and served as a captain of artillery.[109]

As a serviceman in the U.S. military during World War I, Truman's ability to remain calm under pressure came to light. In Truman's first violent encounter during the Great War, German artillery rained down on him and his fellow soldiers. Truman's men panicked. Many of Truman's men frantically began regressing from their battle positions. Meanwhile, Truman was thrown from his horse. To make matters worse, his horse fell on top of him. Truman was temporally stuck. In the midst of the chaos, Truman wiggled himself from underneath his horse and got up. Then, he immediately unleashed a profanity-laced tirade on his men. He demanded they hold the line and continue fighting. Harry Vaughan, close friend and military aide to Truman, once said the future President of the United States was, "One tough son-of-a-bitch of a man... And that

---

[106] Ibid.
[107] Ibid.
[108] Ibid.
[109] Ibid.

was a part of the secret of understanding him."[110] Truman was no coward. He did not crack under pressure. He was fearless and resilient to a fault.

When World War I was over, Truman began his political career. However, to be successful in politics in Kansas City, Missouri, an endorsement from Tom Pendergast's political machine was necessary. Kansas City in the 1920s and 1930s was exceptional, and not necessarily in a good way. Pendergast attempted to construct an image of being an upright leader who was hard on crime. As he put it, "We won't have anything to do with helping drug peddlers or prostitutes. We put the whole strength of the organization to work to slug those people. And to slug them hard."[111] In truth, Kansas City was a cross between Rio De Janeiro, New Orleans and Las Vegas. Smoke-filled jazz clubs featuring famous jazz musicians like Charlie Parker, brothels with prostitutes and gambling parlors lined 12th Street in Kansas City. The puppet master behind this blatant corruption and criminality was not some fat, well dressed gangster with a stogie in his mouth and a woman or two on his lap. Nope. Pendergast, Chairman of the Jackson County Democratic Party, oversaw this massive, sophisticated system of corruption.

Pendergast was a larger-than-life figure in Kansas City politics. He was direct and forthright. He had an oval-shaped head and a no-nonsense

---

[110] David McCullough, "Character Above All: Harry S. Truman Essay," *Public Broadcasting Service*, accessed on Monday, July 25th, 2022, https://www.pbs.org/newshour/spc/character/essays/truman.html.

[111] Kelsey Carls, "'The Social Evil in Kansas City': Machine Politics and the Red Light District," *The Kansas City Public Library*, accessed on Wednesday, December 28th, 2020, https://pendergastkc.org/article/social-evil-kansas-city-machine-politics-and-red-light-district.

demeanor, although at times he could flash a megawatt smile which could light up a room. He wore custom-made suits, smoked cigarettes with an elegant holder and wore a large top hat.[112] Pendergast was akin to a living, breathing God in Kansas City. He had money. He had tremendous political clout. He had status. He controlled the city council, a large army of patronage workers, the allocation of city jobs, numerous businesses which secured lucrative government contracts and forged an alliance with organized crime.[113]

Pendergast was more than an influential force in politics and government in Kansas City. He also managed the dark underbelly of Kansas City which was lathered in corruption and vice. Pendergast charged prostitution rings, gambling halls and drug dealers for protection. Pendergast's command over the Kansas City police force through kickbacks and bribes meant law enforcement was nonexistent. Gambling operations ran efficiently. Prostitutes administered sexual favors in dark alleys, seedy motels and abandoned warehouses without fear of police arresting them. Patrons of nightclubs smelling of fine tobacco, whiskey and cheap beer could openly buy marijuana, heroin, cocaine and amphetamines. If you were a criminal or an up-and-coming politician like Truman in Kansas City in the 1930s and you aligned yourself with the Pendergast machine,

---

[112]   Terence O'Malley, "T.J. Pendergast: A Man in Full," YouTube Video, October 25th, 2015, Tom & Harry: The Boss and the President Documentary Film, 5:28, https://www.youtube.com/watch?v=-FaA3irKc2DQ.

[113]   Kelsey Carls, "'The Social Evil in Kansas City': Machine Politics And The Red-Light District," *The Kansas City Public Library*, Wednesday, December 28th, 2020, https://pendergastkc.org/article/social-evil-kansas-city-machine-politics-and-red-light-district.

you undoubtedly would be rewarded with money, protection and upward mobility within the political establishment.

Kansas City in the early 1920s and 1930s marked the convergence of two worlds coming together — one legitimate and one illegal - which gave birth to a city which was a political and economic juggernaut. Ironically, Kansas City would prove to be an ideal environment for Truman to sharpen his political skills, widen his network within the business community and enhance his influence in political circles on the local, state and federal levels. The veins and arteries which comprised the vascular system of Pendergast's machine were essential to Truman's political future. The machine's reach extended into every nook and cranny of Kansas City. Truman used the Pendergast machine to achieve his political goals. Money, connections, political mentoring and access to Pendergast's vast political army gave Truman a distinct advantage when he entered politics. As he put it, "You cannot get anywhere in politics around Kansas City unless you work within the machine."[114] So, with the backing of the Pendergast machine in 1922, Truman ran for and won a seat on the county court.[115]

Truman's prominence quickly grew within the infamous Pendergast machine. As judge of Jackson County, he earned a reputation for being industrious, honest and efficient.[116] He was well-liked, respected by his colleagues and soon was considered to be a valued member of the

---

[114]   Mark S. Byrnes, *The Truman Years* (London: Routledge Press, 2000), 2.
[115]   Byrnes, *The Truman Years*, 2.
[116]   Ibid.

Kansas City political establishment. The alliance worked. Truman needed the Pendergast machine to help him win reelection and the Kansas City machine needed Truman to represent its interests once he got elected. This symbiotic relationship would continue to pay off for Truman.

In 1934, Truman was nominated to the U.S. Senate.[117] When Truman arrived in Washington, D.C. as the junior senator from Missouri, he was relatively unknown outside of his home state. Things would change within a few years, though. Truman would eventually meet and interact with influential political leaders from across Missouri and throughout the country. As his political profile continued to grow, Truman became less dependent on the Pendergast machine. And, in 1939 the Kansas City machine, which cleared a path for Truman's rise to power, met its fate. Pendergast was convicted of income tax evasion and sent to jail.[118] The imprisonment of Kansas City's infamous political icon marked the end of one of the most influential political machines in U.S. history.

Meanwhile, Truman's political fortunes continued to improve. In 1940 Truman's down-to-earth, Midwestern charm helped him get reelected to the Senate. Truman's reelection suggested he now had a large statewide base which eclipsed the political power generated by the Pendergast machine. Like a snake shedding its skin, Truman was able to shake off his past and reinvent himself. In doing so, Truman's reelection caught the eyes of other bosses within the Democratic Party. In their eyes,

---

[117] Ibid.

[118] Ibid., 3.

Truman had become his own man. He now had a strong, independent political presence. Pegged as an up-and-coming politician, Truman was selected to serve on the Senate's Defense Investigating Committee.[119] He again earned praise for being tough but fair when he allocated resources.[120] At this point, Truman's political stature indicated he was ready to serve in the executive branch of government.[121]

In 1944, Vice President Henry Wallace's dwindling popularity with both the southern wing of the Democratic Party and big city bosses encouraged President Roosevelt to look for a new running mate.[122] He wanted a winner, not a washed-up politician who had fallen out of favor with powerful factions within the Democratic Party. President Roosevelt's advisors sought to find a new candidate who was less controversial and more reliable. Truman seemed like the perfect fit. He embraced New Deal liberalism, had a refreshing Midwestern sensibility which was hard to dislike and a strong, steady presence which reflected an inner confidence. He was revered for his leadership on the Defense Investigating Committee. And, he was popular with numerous political factions, many with opposing views from one another on key issues, within the Democratic Party.[123] After President Roosevelt and his advisors discussed who within the Democratic Party could help the aging political giant win an unprecedented fourth term, President Roosevelt's political campaign

---

[119] Ibid.
[120] Ibid.
[121] Ibid.
[122] Ibid.
[123] Ibid.

decided on Truman. At the Democratic National Convention, Truman was nominated to be President Roosevelt's running mate. The move to put Truman on the ticket proved to be a wise one. With Truman's help, President Roosevelt soundly defeated Republican challenger Thomas Dewey. Truman now was Vice President of the United States, one step away from the Oval Office.

When President Roosevelt took office in 1945, he was tired and worn out. His magnetic smile, warm and supremely confident personality and healthy pinkish-white skin had now been replaced with a stern look, bags under his eyes, dry skin and weight loss. President Roosevelt looked more like a zombie than a living, breathing vibrant human in 1945. To be fair, he had been through a lot since he took office in the early 1930s. He spear-headed the formation of a number of programs like the Works Progress Administration which put Americans back to work. He injected confidence into the American public through his famous fireside chat speeches which were broadcast across the country. He helped Great Britain stay in the war against Nazi Germany with the Lend-Lease Act, a clever program which allowed the United States to give much needed aid to Great Britain and other allies while also maintaining its status as a neutral country at the outset of World War II. And, he oversaw the unleashing of American industriousness and ingenuity as it manufactured an incredible number of tanks, bullets, airplanes and jeeps at breakneck speed. The mass production of these weapons overwhelmed Nazi Germany and Imperial Japan.

So, bearing the responsibility of leading the United States out of the Great Depression and waging a war against Nazi Germany and Imperial Japan had taken its toll on President Roosevelt. The President was on the brink of exhaustion. Beyond that, he was gravely ill. In addition to polio, which left him confined to a wheelchair, President Roosevelt was now suffering from a range of medical conditions. He had arteriosclerosis, which was a hardening of the arteries with plaque buildup. He suffered from acute bronchitis, which caused his chest to tighten and led to a persistent dry cough which kept him up at night. He suffered from high blood pressure and heart failure.[124] Like an old, weathered prizefighter who had taken one too many punches to the head, Roosevelt's health issues were getting the best of him. The political titan was dying. In a matter of months after taking office in 1945, one of America's best presidents would take his last breath, ushering in President Truman as the new leader of the free world.

As President, Truman was faced with a number of issues, including civil rights for African-Americans. When he came to office, he embodied a kind of idealism rooted in the notion that the welfare of the people should be above politics.[125] President Truman's devotion to helping all people became more complicated when he was faced with real social and racial issues. For example, a strike which shut down Capital Transit Company

---

[124]   Tim Ott, "How Franklin Roosevelt's Health Affected His Presidency," *Biography*, Wednesday, December 28th, 2020, https://www.biography.com/news/franklin-roosevelt-health.

[125]   Robert Shogan, *Harry Truman and the Struggle for Racial Justice* (Lawrence: University of Kansas Press, 2013), 1.

(CTC) in November 1946 gave President Truman a chance to take a stance against discrimination. Instead, he avoided the issue of discrimination and seized the company.[126] President Truman had an opportunity to support an order from the Fair Employment Practices Committee which demanded CTC stop discrimination.[127] Charles Hudson, a noted member of the Fair Employment Practices Committee and an African-American, wrote a letter to President Truman encouraging him to support the committee's stance against CTC. President Truman again refused.

In addition to disrespecting the African-American community in politics, President Truman aggravated the African-American community by patronizing venues designated only for Whites. President Truman, the first lady and his daughter Margaret went to Washington's National Theater to watch Sigmund Romberg's schmaltzy musical entitled My Romance.[128] As the presidential limousine drove up to the theater, Secret Service agents started to push away protestors enraged the President of the United States would see a play at a Whites-only theater.[129] When President Truman was asked about the situation, he smugly replied, "I wanted to see the show."[130] Later, he said, "I wanted to see it for twenty years. So I went down there and saw it."[131] President Truman's attendance at the show, coupled with his dismissive explanation of why he went, created

---

[126] Shogan, *Harry Truman and the Struggle for Racial Justice*, 1.
[127] Ibid., 86.
[128] Ibid., 94.
[129] Ibid., 94 – 95.
[130] Ibid.
[131] Ibid.

resentment within the African-American community. In this instance, his desire for entertainment superseded his commitment to take a stand against racial inequality.

While this insult was an affront to the African-American community, it did not affect in a significant way President Truman's push to advance civil rights. He did, in fact, seek to help African-Americans gain their full rights. President Truman authorized the creation of the President's Committee on Civil Rights in 1946.[132] He stated, "Today, freedom from fear and the Democratic institutions which sustain it are again under attack."[133] The President wanted to address this problem by having this committee develop recommendations which would be acted upon by the U.S. government. President Truman believed this committee would aid in protecting civil rights for people in the United States by coming up with real, meaningful solutions to address racial inequality.[134] The President's Committee on Civil Rights signaled his commitment to protecting the rights of African-Americans.

Further, President Truman's devotion to helping African-Americans secure their rights was underscored by his influence on key court decisions. His appointment of Chief Justice Fred Vinson and Associate Justice Harold Burton, both judges sympathetic to the plight of the African-American community, passed important court rulings which were in

---

[132] Ibid., 94.
[133] Ibid.
[134] Ibid.

favor of the civil rights movement.[135] These rulings addressed elements of deep systemic racism which ensured African-Americans could only buy homes in certain areas, were barred from Whites-only bathrooms, could only watch movies in Black-only sections of theaters and ride buses and trains in areas designated only for African-Americans.

President Truman's hand-picked judges successfully championed the cause of civil rights through their court rulings. They were warriors quietly whittling away at White supremacy entrenched in American law. Of the many cases which President Truman's justice department focused on, their work on segregation within elementary schools had the most lasting effect on American society. Attorney Elman, representative of the U.S. government, set out to attack "separate but equal" within the schools by first undermining the legitimacy of the legal doctrine.[136] He did this by suggesting "separate but equal" was inherently contradictory in nature.[137] The separate washrooms, buses, water fountains and education African-Americans and Whites received ensured equality for African-Americans was unobtainable.[138] In effect, Elman peeled back the outer layer of skin of "separate but equal" and discovered an aggressive form of cancer had burrowed into the connective tissue and sweat glands of American society. "Separate but equal" was not making America stronger or better. It was instead gradually killing America from within.

---

[135] Ibid., 168.
[136] Ibid., 176.
[137] Ibid.
[138] Ibid., 176 – 177.

Because segregation within schooling was a heated topic, Elman had to calibrate his argument in a way that would not create social unrest. He knew if he pushed too hard conservative, racist elements within the White community would be agitated. Whites who had little social or political capital could at least revel in the fact they had all of the privileges associated with being White. All White people regardless of social class could drink from the same water fountains, go to the same schools and sit in the front of buses and trains. Elman realized attacking "separate but equal" was attacking the only thing less affluent White people had — their skin. In their minds, they might be poor and uneducated, but at least they were not African-American, a group of people deemed undesirable and valueless in the eyes of most White people in the 1940s. Attacking "separate but equal" could enrage White supremacists and lead to violence, so Elman had to proceed with caution as he sought to dismantle this incredibly racist legal doctrine.

Ending "separate but equal" in a way that did not uproot the racial hierarchy was not the only challenge President Truman's administration faced. The issue of integrating the U.S. military proved to be difficult, especially in America in the 1940s. Jim Crow was still King. African-Americans were still subjected to an onslaught of systematic racism which left deep scars on their psyches and robbed them of a chance to provide a good quality of life for themselves and their families. In spite of this reality, something was changing within the collective soul of the African-American community. African-Americans began to gradually translate their anger and frustration into an organized civil rights movement. Randolph's success in creating the Brotherhood of Sleeping Car Porters in 1925 and in getting President Roosevelt to sign Executive Order 8802, which banned discrimination in government and defense industry employment, indicated Randolph was gathering momentum in his fight to secure equality for African-Americans. He was forcing America to recognize the merits of the civil rights movement. Above all, Randolph's victories demonstrated African-Americans were learning how to advocate for themselves in a way that would bring them real, meaningful change. They now could envision a future filled with hope and opportunity.

As African-Americans became more confident, they also became more irritated over segregation in the U.S. military. Many African-American men were just as patriotic as White men. They believed in protecting democracy and they wanted America to give them a chance to prove it on the battlefield. The symbolism of African-American and White soldiers fighting alongside each other for democracy and freedom was just the ointment America needed to heal from the deep, gaping wound left behind by slavery. African-American men serving in the U.S. military alongside White soldiers could bring America together, once and for all unifying America.

However, this sentiment was not embraced by everyone. Some people believed the status quo should remain the same in the U.S. military. Men like Lieutenant General Almond believed African-Americans were inferior. He believed African-American soldiers should continue to play a supporting role in the U.S. military. Some White youth, especially from the South, could not see themselves fighting in a foxhole alongside an African-American soldier. Many White soldiers from the South were marinated in a stew of hate towards African-Americans. So, the very concept of African-American soldiers serving in an integrated U.S. military shattered the myth they were not mentally strong enough, noble enough or courageous enough to fight with White soldiers. Nevertheless, many White soldiers would change their minds once they started to serve with African-American soldiers.[139] Most White soldiers wisely came to the conclusion survival reigned supreme during battle. A bullet from an enemy's gun did not check to see if its target was White or African-American. A majority of White soldiers determined if they wanted to increase their odds of making it out alive from the battlefields of Korea they had to put aside their prejudices and work with African-American soldiers to survive. It was common sense.

In the end, President Truman signed into law Executive Order 9981. President Truman, however, did not sign Executive Order 9981 after experiencing some moral epiphany in the middle of the night. He did not have some dream where he was transplanted into the body of an African-American man who was being beaten into a messy, mushy soup of blood, urine, feces, fragments of bone and skin tissue by members of the Ku Klux Klan. Instead, his decision to end segregation in the U.S. mili-

---

[139]   Ibid., 140.

tary was driven by politics. The Democratic Party was fragmented, with Dixiecrats on the right and progressives led by Henry Wallace on the left.[140] To win the 1948 election against Republican Governor Thomas Dewey, President Truman needed the African-American community's support.[141] So, after some cajoling by Randolph, President Truman gave in to his demands for integrating the U.S. military. He issued Executive Order 9981, which established the President's Committee on Equality of Treatment and Opportunity in the Armed Services.[142] Due to the creation of this committee, President Truman was given recommendations on how to integrate African-Americans into the U.S. military.

The combination of a fractured Democratic Party and political pressure from Randolph encouraged President Truman to desegregate the U.S. military. Randolph was a brilliant social activist. He knew how to negotiate with powerful White men like President Roosevelt and President Truman to create real, meaningful change for African-Americans. Randolph's work on integrating the U.S. military proved civil disobedience could help African-Americans secure their rights. Indeed, his efforts laid the foundation for the passage of the Voting Rights Act which was enacted in 1965. Also, his campaign to desegregate the U.S. military trained future African-American civil rights leaders. Men like Bayard Rustin, an exceptional civil rights strategist, drew inspiration from Randolph's social activism. Civil rights leaders saw his mental toughness and determination

---

[140]   Ibid., 146.
[141]   Ibid.
[142]   Ibid., 146 – 147.

as he stared down the powerful Pullman Company. They witnessed his political savvy on full display when he negotiated with President Roosevelt on African-Americans securing government and defense industry jobs.[143] And, they saw him emerge victorious after confronting President Truman on desegregating the U.S. military. To many African-Americans, Randolph was more than just a mere mortal. He was a Black Moses who parted the Red Sea tainted with the blood of White supremacy for African-Americans. In doing so, Randolph was instrumental in igniting a fire of civic activism which would continue throughout the 1960s and beyond.

White supremacy was tightly interwoven into the DNA of the U.S. military in the 1940s. The U.S. military, especially the high command, was filled with a ton of White males who were diehard supporters of maintaining the racial hierarchy within the U.S. military. These were the type of guys which could be mean-spirited, but were as reliable as a Ford pickup truck: tough, dependable, resolute and smart. They were not easily intimidated. Moreover, these types of men were not afraid of death in the same way most people are. They made their peace with it. They would rather sacrifice themselves defending a friend, a family member or themselves rather than to surrender.

Alpha males such as Lieutenant General Almond and General MacArthur were stubborn and forthright in their convictions. They were tough, disciplined guys who were taught at some of America's finest military academies like West Point and the U.S. Naval Academy. They stood

---

[143]   Ibid., 167.

tall, remained focused and calm under pressure, and, above all, respected U.S. military protocol and procedures. These types of leaders within the U.S. military believed separation of African-American and White soldiers was just how the U.S. military functioned, a key organizing principle of this powerful and influential American institution. More than that, they believed African-American soldiers were inferior to White soldiers. When President Truman signed Executive Order 9981, many racist White commanding officers and average White soldiers were enraged. They felt the U.S. military was going to hell. In their minds, African-American soldiers would weaken all White infantry units and, in doing so, make the U.S. military less efficient and less effective in waging war.

They were wrong. The implementation of "separate but equal" within the U.S. military was incredibly expensive, time consuming and hard to maintain. The construction of separate barracks, mess halls, bathrooms and training facilities for African-American and White soldiers was financially draining. U.S. military leaders such as Lieutenant General Almond, General MacArthur and others were stuck in the past. Due to their racism, they could not comprehend how integration of the U.S. military would strengthen the U.S. Armed Forces. Therefore, their bigotry and intransigence proved to be a liability because it prevented the U.S. military from evolving into a better, stronger and more cohesive institution.

These prevailing racist sentiments both inside and outside of the U.S. military magnified the importance of Randolph's victory over desegregating the U.S. military. Through his efforts, a door was cracked open for African-Americans looking to serve their country in the U.S. military. Soon African-American soldiers would squeeze through that door and enlist in the U.S. military. These men would go on to prove themselves as battle-hardened warriors, willing and able to kill and, if necessary, die for their country at the blink of an eye.

CHAPTER 2

Preparation

Jesse Brown ran up to his brother, Marvin, and asked, "Can I get a dime?" Marvin, being the good brother he was, obliged. Marvin knew Brown wanted badly to see *Hell's Angels*, which had just come out in the movie theaters. Brown grabbed the money out of his brother's hand and ran right out the door and toward the movie theater. *Hell's Angels*, the larger-than-life movie production which used 137 airplanes and one Zeppelin airship in two dynamic air combat scenes, was playing at the Saenger Theater in downtown Hattiesburg, Mississippi.[144]

The Saenger Theater was more like a public palace than an actual theater. It was the crown jewel of the downtown area for Hattiesburg, a medium sized city in Mississippi, one of the poorest states in the United States. Built in the Neoclassical style, the theater was breathtaking. It had ornate light fixtures and beautiful high ceilings, and a kind of magnetic power which drew people from around the surrounding area of Harris-

---

[144]   Theodore Taylor, *The Flight of Jesse Leroy Brown* (Annapolis: Naval Institute Press, 1998), 25 – 26.

burg to it. It made people feel special when they entered the space. Brown's dream of seeing *Hell's Angels* at the Saenger Theater amplified the movie experience for him.

When Brown arrived at the theater, he saw the large and brightly lit Saenger marquee. It brought a huge smile to his face. Brown bought his ticket and walked through the entrance past the front facade. He marveled at the huge glistening chandelier. As he was staring at the chandelier, he could not help but witness a mother grab her five-year-old son and quickly move him from underneath the shimmering cake-like light fixture, concerned it might fall on him. Brown turned his head and gazed at the gorgeous tile fountain next to the men's restroom. When he made his way up the stairs to the Blacks-only section in the balcony, he settled into his plush upholstered seat.

As Brown waited for the movie to begin, music blared from the organ in the theater. The music was a nice distraction as the theater production crew were preparing to start the movie. Suddenly, the organ stopped, the lights went out, the curtains were drawn back and *Hell's Angels* began. Brown watched attentively as Roy and Monte Rutledge, two brothers who were attending Oxford University, competed for the attention of Helen. Both men joined the Royal Flying Corps and engaged the German Air Force in air combat. In the end, the two brothers went on a daring mission to raid a German munitions dump which eventually got both of them killed.[145] As Brown watched the movie, he envisioned himself picking up a machine gun and firing at the German airplanes. Brown absorbed the visual imagery and message in *Hell's Angels*. He could not help but long for the chance when he could fly his own plane and defend his country in air combat. Brown wanted to be a fighter pilot, a profession which was little more than a dream for African-Americans during the Great Depression.

Most African-Americans, especially in southern states like Mississippi, were sharecroppers. Many African-Americans were poor farmers who rented small parcels of land owned by White landowners. As a form of payment for using their land, African-American sharecroppers gave a part of their crop yield to the White landlord. Despite the name sharecropping implying equity, parity, fairness and collaboration, this could not be further from the truth. Sharecropping was a variation of slavery, a system designed to exploit African-Americans for labor while bringing in huge profit margins for the White people who owned the land. Sharecropping was catastrophic for African-Americans because the system robbed them of a chance to own their own land and, above all, to be the masters of their own fates. Instead, African-American sharecroppers were forced to remain dependent on White landowners for their economic survival.

The system of sharecropping was a clever way to reintroduce slavery into the fabric of the southern way of life without the racial and historical connotations linked to the word slavery. Sharecropping put Afri-

---

[145]   Peter Jakab, "Hell's Angels: Hughes' Big Crash and Harlow's Big Break," *Smithsonian: National Air and Space Museum*, Wednesday, December 28th, 2020, https://airandspace.si.edu/stories/editorial/hells-angels.

can-Americans back on a treadmill of forced labor which they could not get off of, leaving many drowning in debt and poverty stricken. Like being stuck in a nightmare which goes on and on and on, sharecropping was a reminder that African-Americans were still vulnerable to economic exploitation, even after the defeat of the Confederacy during the Civil War.

John Brown, Jesse's father, knew all too well the inherent racism of sharecropping. John rented thirty acres of land from Joe Ingram, a slender White man. John was built like a tank, with a big, brawny chest and well defined, strong arms. He had a steady gaze indicative of his natural confidence. He, along with his sons, worked countless hours chopping down trees, pulling mules and planting seeds. If he needed new tools or seeds, he was required to buy them from Ingram. At the end of the year, John gave a portion of his crops to Ingram, wiping away the yearly profit the Brown family made.[146] John was aware of the inconvenient truth he never could quite turn a profit. He felt trapped. He wanted to break Ingram's nose and snap his little neck in half, leaving his lifeless body in a pool of blood. But he did not act on these urges, even though these feelings were justified.

Not only was John's family subjected to economic exploitation in Mississippi, but the racism he and his family faced was reprehensible. Racism was like COVID-19 in Mississippi during the Great Depression. Bigotry lingered in the air waiting to come out from the shadows and blindside African-Americans. While John and his family were walking home after a long day of working the fields in the hot, humid Mississippi

---

[146]   Adam Makos, *Devotion* (New York: Ballantine Books, 2015), 19 - 21.

sun, his son Fletcher wanted to relax a little, unwind and have some fun. So, Fletcher asked Jesse to ask their father, John, if they could go swimming in a pond in the forest. John obliged and told his children they could take a break as long as they completed their chores when they got home.[147]

John's children abruptly ran towards the entrance of a wooded trail which snaked through a forest. They could hear the crickets. They saw lighting bugs, grasshoppers and squirrels scattered throughout the forest. They were on the lookout for cottonmouths, long venomous snakes which could survive on land or in water. When they got to the middle of the woods, they came to a dirty, scummy pond. They took off their sweaty clothes and immediately jumped in. They laughed, yelled, slashed water on each other and screamed with delight as they swam in the pond. Their sounds kept the cottonmouth snakes away. This was their time to let loose and be themselves. When they finished swimming, they got out of the pond, dried off, put their clothes back on and then made their way back to the road which led to their house.[148]

As John's children were walking down the road, they could hear the faint rumble of a vehicle in the distance. As they continued to walk, the noise became louder and more distinct. Jesse Brown and his younger brothers could now identify the noise — it was a school bus. The road they were walking on was narrow and thin, so Brown escorted Fletcher and Lura over to the side of the road. They could now hear the winding down

---

[147]   Makos, *Devotion*, 19.
[148]   Ibid., 21 – 22.

of the gears and the revving of the engine coming from the bus. Brown again gently moved his brothers further to the side of the road. He wanted to make sure the bus had enough room to get by them.[149]

The school bus made it around the corner and slowly approached Brown and his brothers. The bus had black paint on its nose and bright yellow paint on its side. It also had large, robust tires, which supported the vehicle's long rectangular frame. As the bus rattled closer to them, Brown and his two siblings could see the windows were down. White heads were bobbing in the air. Boys with short sandy brown hair and others with curly blond hair and White girls with jet black hair were sticking their heads out their windows, taking in the fresh, humid Mississippi air. The White kids on the bus turned their attention to Brown and his brothers and shouted, "Heya niggers!" "Dirty niggers!" "Look here, niggers!" The White kids burst out laughing, reveling in the delight of humiliating Brown and his two younger brothers.[150]

Then, the White kids spit from their mouths a cluster of brownish white phlegm onto Brown and his siblings. They tried to cover their faces, but the sheer magnitude and concentration of saliva launched at them ensured some of it got into the boys' mouths, eyes, ears and hair. Some of the saliva even landed on their bare chests and arms. The liquid discharge raining down on them felt like the torrential thunderstorms which often swept across Florida during the spring and summer months.[151] The storms

---

[149]   Ibid., 22 – 23.

[150]   Ibid., 23.

[151]   Ibid.

63

move in fast, briefly let loose living hell on anyone and anything in their path, and just as quickly leave the scene of the crime. Dust, the smell of hot diesel emanating from the bus and the sticky, humid weather added further insult to the excruciating pain the boys were already experiencing. As the bus rumbled past them, they could hear the White children laughing, giggling and hollering as if it was one big fat joke. The disgusting, mean-spirited White students made Brown and his brothers feel as though they were worth less than poop from the mules their father got from Ingram's supply store.[152]

The racism Brown and his brothers experienced was wrong on so many levels. Their excursion into the woods and swimming in a secluded pond should have been the crowning moment of their day. It should have brought them joy, happiness and relaxation. Instead, the White students' racist venom, coupled with the barrage of spit they hurled at Brown and his siblings, brought them anger and humiliation. In spite of the racism Brown was subjected to early on in his life, he would persevere to achieve his goals.

One of Brown's crowing achievements in life was his successful courtship of Daisy Nix. Daisy was gorgeous. She was tall and slender, with high cheekbones and a chestnut brown complexion. She had great posture and a quiet disposition. And, she was graceful.[153] When Brown met Daisy, he knew he wanted to get to know her better. Unbeknownst

---

[152]   Ibid.

[153]   Ibid., 46 – 47.

to Brown, Daisy was just as interested in him as he was into her. In fact, she was in hot pursuit of him. He just did not know it. Brown was a good catch. He was a great student. He was the highest ranked math student in his junior class. Beyond academics, he was an excellent athlete, thriving as a runner and long jumper. Finally, Brown was handsome. He was tall, somewhat lanky and muscular. And, he had a nice, inviting smile which put people at ease.[154]

Every day, Daisy and her girlfriends would purposely eat lunch near Brown's woodshop class, trying to get him to notice them. Daisy would try to get Brown's attention without appearing desperate. The trap was set. Brown was shy and had never been on a date before. Since he was a top student at Eureka High School, he spent most of his time on homework, not chasing girls. Like most high school boys, he had raging hormones and kept his eyes open for the cutest, finest girl who piqued his interest. As he put it, "I was an excellent girlwatcher. And she was the one I had my eye on."[155] Daisy, however, had her eye on her man, too. They would eventually meet, go out on dates and, ultimately, fall in love.

Brown's adoration for Daisy was evident in the beautiful love letters he wrote to her. When he could not spend time with her in person outside of school, he wrote long, detailed letters and sent them via special delivery to her house. These letters ensured the connection between Brown and Daisy remained strong, even when they were not able to see each other.

---

[154]   Ibid., 36.

[155]   Ibid., 47.

They expressed his deep commitment to her, the trials and tribulations he endured daily and, above all, his gritty determination to achieve his objectives.

When Brown was admitted to Ohio State University, he was entering the world of academia, a place filled with a new set of challenges which he would have to face as an African-American male. Brown would be the only African-American person in many of his classes. He would be isolated, scrutinized and vilified all for being an African-American male. Since African-Americans were not allowed to live on campus, he was forced to find housing elsewhere.

To make matters worse, Brown also was struggling financially to stay in school. Brown's deep desire to achieve his goals, even if it meant almost working himself to death, energized him. In Mississippi before he left for Ohio State, Brown worked as a department store janitor. He swept and mopped floors, took out the trash, washed windows and cleaned urine-stained bathrooms. He also worked at the Holmes Club, a saloon for White soldiers. He got paid six dollars a night. On his last night, the bar owner sent his hat around to all of the White soldiers to raise money for Brown. Men dug into their pockets and threw wads of cash into the hat. Dollar bills mixed in with fives, tens and twenties filled the hat. Money which would have gone to buying groceries for their own families or to put gas in their own pickup trucks, instead went to Brown's scholarship fund for college. The bar owner raised over seven hundred dollars for Brown, which was enough for an entire year's tuition. The White bar owner was a nice, caring guy. He did not see Brown as just another man who worked for him. He saw a human. He looked past Brown's race and saw a young man barely scrapping by who needed a little extra help to survive.[156]

When Brown got to Ohio State, his financial problems continued. He joined track and field, a sport he thrived at in high school, but was forced to quit and get another job so he could stay in school. Despite his father not giving Brown a penny, he managed to work a job which gave him just enough money to continue his studies at Ohio State. Brown worked loading and unloading engine parts on boxcars from 3:30 p.m. to 12 a.m.[157] The backbreaking manual labor required for his job was punishing his body. He told Daisy in one of his many letters to her, "I very seldom pick up anything weighing less than eighty pounds."[158] He made eighty-three cents per hour.[159] After working through most of the night, Brown came home, did his homework, took a shower and slept for a few hours. When he woke, he would often feel drowsy and tired. As he slowly rose from his bed, he was met with aches and pains from the heavy lifting of engine parts he was required to do at his job the night before. Nevertheless, Brown would fight through the pain, put on his clothes, grab some breakfast, quickly gulp down a cup of hot coffee and head to class.

---

[156] Ibid., 47 – 48.
[157] Theodore Taylor, *The Flight of Jesse Leroy Brown* (Annapolis: Naval Institute Press, 1998), 16.
[158] Taylor, *The Flight of Jesse Leroy Brown*, 16.
[159] Ibid.

Brown's financial difficulties were not the only problem he faced at Ohio State. Various forms of racism at Ohio State proved to be yet another challenge he would have to confront. Though the first African-American student had graduated from Ohio State in 1888, racism was still deeply entrenched in the fabric of the school in the mid to late 1940s. African-Americans were not valued by the faculty, staff or student body. African-American students would often sit in a corner during lunch, largely ignored by their White peers. Some White students would stare at African-American students when they entered a classroom as though they had lesions on their skin from leprosy. Other White students would study them as if they were lab rats. Some White students would scrutinize comments made by African-American students during class, looking for ways to discredit and delegitimatize their ideas and arguments. Still other White students would analyze their body language, looking for anything that seemed peculiar or abnormal to them. When class was over, some White students would go back to their dorm rooms and ridicule African-American students' hair, clothes, skin complexion, body movements and intellectual contributions to class discussions.

To make matters worse, there was not a critical mass of African-American students on Ohio State's campus in the 1940s. So, African-American students could not draw strength from their community. African-American students on college campuses in the United States in the 1940s were like rare wild buffalo on the open prairie out West. One African-American student who attended the University in the 1940s recalls not seeing more than one hundred African-American people.[160] And, the University's treatment of the few African-Americans who were admitted was criminal. They were not even allowed to live on campus until the 1950s. Instead, most African-American students were forced to live off campus, oftentimes miles away from where their classes were being held. The message sent to African-American students was undeniable. Ohio State wanted African-American students to know they were, in fact, not a part of the school. They were not viewed by the University as valued commodities, but instead as barely tolerated junk bonds.

Ohio State's curriculum also reflected institutional racism. Some African-Americans thought the curriculum was too focused on extolling the values and beliefs of Western civilization, while either ignoring or minimizing the contributions Africans, Asians and Latinos made to art, science, math and philosophy. One African-American student who went to Ohio State in the 1940s remembered the Psychology Department refused to admit any African-Americans into the program.[161] This stance was detrimental to the quality of education provided in the department. African-Americans could have enriched class dialogues on course content, providing new and different perspectives on concepts presented during class. However, the department's racist position on not allowing African-Americans into the department guaranteed this would not take place.

---

[160]   "The Hidden History of Ohio State's Black Student Body," Ohio State University, accessed December 28, 2021, https://odi.osu.edu/hidden-history-ohio-states-black-student-body.

[161]   Ibid.

Given the stifling racism Brown experienced at Ohio State, he jumped at the opportunity to enroll in a new aviation program sponsored by the U.S. Navy. When Brown came across a Navy poster advertising a new aviation program, he reached out to Lieutenant Earl Dawkins, a recruiting officer for the V-5 Naval Aviation Program, to express his interest in joining.[162] Brown believed this could be the big chance he was waiting for to make his dream of becoming a fighter pilot a reality. He could visualize getting into his own airplane, taking a deep breath and smelling wafts of engine fuel in the air. He could imagine his heart beating faster with excitement. He could picture himself taking off and engaging in intense dogfights with battle-hardened German fighter pilots. He could feel the uneasiness of walking on a tightrope which divided life from death. One false move, one mistake and the German fighter pilot could blow him into bite-sized chunks of flesh, bone and blood. Despite that, Brown envisioned himself fighting through the fear, the pain and anguish and killing all of the German fighter pilots with a mixture of creativity, courage and precision. He could taste it in the air — victory.

Nonetheless, when Brown met Dawkins, his hopes were dashed once again. Dawkins only saw Brown's race and gender, which was all he needed to determine he was not qualified to be a part of the Naval Aviation Program. Dawkins told Brown bluntly, "There has never been an African-American man ever to enter selective flight training. Never."[163]

---

[162]   Adam Makos, *Devotion* (New York: Ballantine Books, 2015), 47.

[163]   Theodore Taylor, *The Flight of Jesse Leroy Brown* (Annapolis: Naval Institute Press, 1998), 17.

Dawkins wanted to clear up any ambiguity for Brown — the Naval Aviation Program was "only" for White males. He probably thought to himself, who the hell is this African-American man coming in here demanding information on an elite aviation program which has been since its inception an exclusive club for White males?

To underscore this point, Dawkins told Brown, "It has been forty years since Eugene Eli put a plane down on a so-called carrier. That is a lot of White pilot tradition. Proud tradition."[164] Dawkins said flight instructors would grade Brown down just because of the color of his skin.[165] Dawkins' words were like taking salt and rubbing it into an open wound on Brown's back. He wanted Brown to feel the pain of being racially excluded. He wanted Brown to feel uneasy and squirm just a little.

In spite of Dawkins' mean-spirited comments which were sprinkled with good old-fashioned bigotry and prejudice, he did not quite slam the door on Brown's dream of becoming a fighter pilot. He left the door cracked just a little, giving Brown a modicum of hope. Dawkins told him if he passed the entrance exam for the Naval Aviation Program he would be admitted into the program. Brown looked at Dawkins and told him, "I like to try, sir. I still like to try."[166] The Lieutenant took a deep breath and shook his head, perplexed at Brown's unwillingness to take no for an answer.

Brown was told he would fail the entrance exam, though like always his perseverance prevailed. He took the exam over and over again until he

---

164   Taylor, *The Flight of Jesse Leroy Brown*, 17.
165   Ibid.
166   Ibid.

passed it. Brown even muddled his way through the five-hour written part of the assessment.[167] Then, he took the Naval Aviation Program's physical the next day and passed with flying colors. After being told time and time again he was not qualified, not quite good enough, not quite smart enough, Brown was finally admitted into the program.

African-Americans who served in the U.S. Navy were fairly common in the late 1940s. Even so, African-American servicemen training to be Navy pilots was unheard of or, for that matter, seen before. U.S. Navy aircraft were off-limits to African-American sailors. Instead, most African-Americans in the Navy were largely relegated to support staff on various types of ships and submarines which comprised the U.S. Navy. African-American soldiers mopped floors. They cleared passageways of debris. They vacuumed carpets, cleaned linen and made the beds for White officers. So, many White servicemen and personnel within the Naval Air Force considered the idea of African-American soldiers flying expensive, sophisticated aircraft as inconceivable. Brown, however, was an exception to the rule.

After being admitted into the Naval Aviation Program, Brown quit Ohio State and was off to Glenview, Illinois for Selective Flight Training. He gathered with the other recruits and waited for the blue and gray bus with large letters which read U.S. Naval Air Training Command to pull up. When the bus arrived, the bus driver slammed on the breaks and swung open the door. Brown eagerly climbed the stairs onto the bus. Before he

---

[167]   Ibid., 18.

could turn the corner and make his way to the back of the vehicle, the African-American bus driver looked Brown in the eyes and said, "Hey, boy, you are on the wrong bus. We goin' to the air base…"[168] The words startled Brown. He expected to experience racism from Whites, not from African-Americans, while he was training to become a Navy pilot. He was beginning to realize racism seeped into virtually every crevice and crack in American society. No one was immune to its toxicity. It affected everyone. It could sprout up in the most unexpected ways. In truth, racism occasionally even came from other people within his own ethnic group.

Brown glared at the bus driver. He thought to himself the bus driver should be ashamed to cast doubt on whether or not he belonged on the bus, especially in front of other White servicemen who most likely had similar concerns. Brown, however, did not make a spectacle. He remained calm. Brown took out his Apprentice Seaman orders and handed them over to the bus driver. The bus driver then took the papers and began to study them, looking for any inconsistency which could suggest the documents were falsified. After a few moments, the bus driver turned to Brown in disbelief. Brown assumed the bus driver was having problems processing the concept that an African-American man could be training to become a Navy pilot. Brown told the bus driver, "They aren't counterfeit." After thoroughly inspecting his documents, the bus driver finally

---

[168] Ibid., 35.

gave them back to Brown and let him on the bus. Brown proceeded to the back of the bus, took a seat and got comfortable.[169]

Once he got settled, Brown turned and stared out the window, marveling at the trees which were on the cusp of springing back to life. He took in the beautiful green foliage. Brown was ready for anything as he encountered the White recruits. He was envisioning some of them ignoring him. Others he thought may give him dirty looks. Still, others might make derogatory comments either under their breath or to his face. He could imagine some would even try to physically assault him just for having the audacity to get on a bus labeled U.S. Naval Air Training Command, a bus which was taking these men down a rabbit hole which would lead to some of them becoming part of an exclusive, all-White male club of elite American fighter pilots.

To Brown's amazement, none of that happened. Instead, Gus Gillespie, a former student from Dartmouth College, an elite private college located in Hanover, New Hampshire, sat down next to him. Gillespie looked over at the Ohio State warm up jacket Brown had on and said, "OSU, huh?"[170] Brown quietly nodded. He did not know what to expect from Gillespie, so he applied the concept of "less is more" under the circumstances. Gillespie then said, "I'm Gus Gillespie, Dartmouth," and extended his hand.

Brown shook his hand and said, "Jesse Brown."

---

169   Ibid.
170   Ibid., 36.

Gillespie said with enthusiasm, "So off we go to be flyboys."

Brown shot back, "Try to!"[171]

When the bus pulled up to the base, all the men got off, checked in, got settled in their rooms and then went to the cafeteria to get some food. Brown's journey toward becoming a Navy fighter pilot had just begun.[172]

Brown began his flight instruction with Lieutenant Roland Christensen, a man from Nebraska who was clean-cut and displayed a no-nonsense professionalism in his work. Brown was the only African-American man up to this point to go through aviation training. In that sense, it made him unique and exceptional, but not necessarily valued. Many flight instructors concluded it was only a matter of time before he would quit the program. Other flight instructors stayed away from Brown because they thought their reputations would be tarnished, especially if he made a huge mistake like crashing a plane.[173]

Given the negative perception of Brown based solely on his race, flight instructors were not clamoring to teach him. However, where many instructors saw Brown as not having a snowball's chance in hell of passing, Christensen saw an opportunity to mold and shape him into a good, capable fighter pilot. So, he walked up to Brown, introduced himself and asked him where he was from.

Brown told him, "Mississippi, sir."[174]

---

[171] Ibid.

[172] Ibid., 36 – 38.

[173] Ibid., 40.

[174] Ibid., 41.

Then, he asked Brown if his family was into farming. Brown said, "Yes."[175]

Christensen replied, "We have something in common. I was born on a dryland prairie farm which my grandparents homesteaded. They lived in a sod house and plowed with oxen."[176] The move was brilliant. In that brief moment, Christensen established contact with his chosen student. His down-to-earth personality put Brown at ease by creating a common thread between them. Christensen turned out to be an angel sent from God for Brown.

Christensen wanted to make sure Brown was prepared before he went off to battle in Korea. He was firm but also exercised patience with him. He set high expectations for Brown and expected him to meet them. No corners would be cut. Brown was first taught key principles of flying an airplane. He learned how thrust, lift, drag and weight affected an aircraft during flight. He gave Brown instructions on how to use the elevator to control the pitch of an airplane. He demonstrated to Brown how to use the rudder to make turns and to manage the vertical axis, which ensured the plane remained steady and that its nose was pointed in the right direction. Christensen taught him how to take off, recover from a stall, and land an airplane. After Brown mastered these concepts, the Lieutenant switched seats with Brown. Brown was now required to put these basic flying principles which Christensen drilled into his head into

---

[175]   Ibid.
[176]   Ibid.

action. Brown did countless loops, sharp turns, rolls, spins, rectangular patterns and emergency landings. Under Christensen's tutelage, Brown's confidence improved. His self-doubt melted away and he began to feel at ease while flying. After all these maneuvers were etched into Brown's memory, Christensen handed over the airplane to him. Brown was ready for solo flights.[177]

Brown started the engine of his airplane and took off. This time Brown did not have Christensen's reassuring voice to help guide him as he flew. He had to rely on himself. Brown effortlessly made tight and wide turns, steep dives, straight climbs and big rolls. He even nailed three perfect landings. On his final landing, Brown picked up the Lieutenant and they flew back to the air station. When they got out of the airplane, Christensen looked Brown in the eye and said, "I am proud of you, Jesse, for a lot of reasons. I honestly think you will be a fine naval aviator."[178] Brown had defied the odds. He did what many others had told him he could not do — become a Navy fighter pilot.

Brown was exceptional for a number of reasons. He refused to allow entrenched racism stop him from achieving his goal of becoming a fighter pilot. Lesser men would have given up. They would have hung their heads down, thrown up their hands and quit. These types of men would have fallen into prevailing stereotypes that African-American men were just not capable of handling asymmetrical warfare at thirty thousand

---

[177]   Ibid., 57.
[178]   Ibid.

feet. Despite encountering various forms of racism at different points in his life, Brown would not be deterred. His determination and focus never wavered. After Brown completed the Naval Aviation Program, he received his gold-metal Naval Aviation Wings. He now was officially a naval aviator.

Luckily, the U.S. military was at a turning point right before the outbreak of the Korean War when Brown was seeking to become the first African-American Navy fighter pilot. With President Truman desegregating the military with Executive Order 9981, on July 26th, 1948, the Korean War provided a unique opportunity for the U.S. military to tear down the walls of segregation which separated African-American and White soldiers. This subtle shift in racial attitudes towards African-Americans within the U.S. military gave Brown a chance to prove himself as a capable fighter pilot within the U.S. Navy. To Brown's credit, he did not squander this once-in-a-lifetime opportunity. Instead, he took this moment in time to crack open the door to the exclusive, all-White club of naval aviators.

Just as Brown struggled to break the glass ceiling in the U.S. Navy Aviation Program, African-American infantry soldiers like Curtis Morrow of the 24th experienced similar challenges. Morrow's basic training experiences were highlighted by a web of complex and contradictory segregation policies on U.S. Army bases which lasted throughout the duration of the Korean War. Despite this, the training African-American soldiers received during the Korean War, especially when compared to that given during World War I and World War II, was the best they had received up to that point in U.S. military history. In spite of racism they endured on a daily basis, men like Morrow from the 24th, were, in fact, ready to meet the demands each soldier was required to carry out during the war.

Before the Korean War, African-American participation in armed conflicts was not necessarily guaranteed. When World War I broke out, Jim Crow laws ensured African-Americans and Whites remained segregated in housing, schooling, restaurants, trains and buses. African-Americans were also denied the right to vote.[179] They were treated as second-class citizens. Understandably, they were angry. Some African-Americans were hesitant to fight for a country which did not value them as humans. Others, however, thought fighting for America would give them greater leverage against racial oppression. They believed if they joined the U.S. military they would get more respect in American society, securing greater equality for the African-American community. W.E.B. DuBois fell into the latter camp. The famed Harvard-educated sociologist and activist urged African-Americans to forget "our special grievances" and support the war effort in Europe during World War I.[180] DuBois's pragmatism was evident.

As DuBois eloquently put it, "Let us not hesitate. Let us, while this war lasts, forget our special grievances and close our ranks shoulder to

---

179 "Jim Crow Laws," Public Broadcasting Station, accessed on August 25, 2020, https://www.pbs.org/wgbh/americanexperience/features/freedom-riders-jim-crow-laws/.
180 W.E.B. DuBois, "Close Ranks," *The Crisis*, July 1918, 111.

shoulder with our own White fellow citizens and the allied nations that are fighting for democracy."[181] DuBois was smart. He knew African-Americans were in a bind. If they failed to enroll in the U.S. military, they would be considered cowards, making it more difficult for the community to secure equal rights. If they did join the U.S. military, they would be disrespected by other White soldiers because they were perceived as inferior soldiers. DuBois reasoned the African-American community had more to gain by serving in the U.S. Armed Forces than deciding not to participate in the war effort. DuBois's efforts to encourage African-Americans to enroll in the U.S. military worked. On July 5th, 1917 over seven hundred thousand African-Americans registered for the U.S. military.[182] African-American men were ready to serve their country during a time of war. The numbers proved it.

African-American soldiers' enthusiasm to serve their country was not reciprocated by the U.S. military. The military did not want them nor value their contribution. President Wilson's interpretation of World War I as a "White man's war" meant African-Americans would only play a nominal role.[183] A cap on the number of African-American men who could enlist in the U.S. Army was established. Beyond that, African-American soldiers who were accepted into the U.S. Armed Forces were subjected to another layer of discrimination — placement. Of the

---

[181]   DuBois, *Close Ranks*, 111.

[182]   Gail Buckley, *American Patriots: The Story of Blacks in the Military from the Revolution to Desert Storm* (New York: Random House Trade Paperbacks, 2001), 165.

[183]   Buckley, *American Patriots: The Story of Blacks in the Military from the Revolution to Desert Storm*, 165.

367,710 African-American draftees who served during World War I, roughly eighty-nine percent of them were assigned to labor, supply and/ or service units.[184] Therefore, most African-American soldiers were not given a chance to prove themselves under fire.

The training African-American soldiers received during World War I was mediocre at best. At this moment in history, the American government saw no value in training African-American soldiers for war. Since most African-American soldiers were either laborers or stevedores in engineer service battalions, the consensus within the U.S. military brass was that training them for combat was a waste of money.[185] African-American soldiers who were given a chance to prove themselves ironically did not fight for America. They fought for France. The 369th and 370th Infantries were praised by French officers and soldiers for their combat skills during battle. Men of the 369th, better known as "Harlem's Hell Fighters," served with distinction alongside French soldiers, earning numerous awards for their accomplishments on the battlefield. So, aside from that which the 369th and 370th received, the training most African-American soldiers received during World War I paled in comparison to what African-American soldiers would later get during the Korean War.

World War I highlighted the U.S. military's efforts to provide more consistency in training for all American soldiers.[186] When the United

---

[184] Ibid.

[185] "African-American Participation During World War I," HCA Delaware Historical and Cultural Affairs, accessed Wednesday, July 29th, https://history.delaware.gov/african-americans-ww1/.

[186] Conrad C. Crane, Michael E. Lynch, Shane P. Reilly, Jessica J. Sheets, *U.S. Army Heritage and Education Center, Learning the Lessons of Lethality: The Army's Cycle of Basic Combat Training, 1918 – 2019*

States entered World War I, the country had to immediately raise an army to fight against the Axis powers (the German Empire, the Austro-Hungarian Empire, the Bulgarian Empire and the Ottoman Empire). The system, however, was riddled with problems as basic training was provided only on the regimental level.

Because the Division Commander was responsible for preparing soldiers for war, the quality of training soldiers received varied. The training focused more on mobilization than actually providing soldiers with skills such as shooting a gun.[187] Finally, drafted men were sent "directly to regiments, which provided rudimentary training to familiarize soldiers with military discipline and operations."[188] Simply put, basic training provided to soldiers during World War I was second-rate.

Deregulation of basic training continued during the interwar period between World War I and World War II. The 1928 regulation emphasized "progressive training," focusing on training the individual as it relates to subdivisions of units from smallest to largest.[189] Above all, "Recruits were to be trained in Articles of War, regulations, orders, customs, physical fitness, hygiene, drill, guard duty, and more."[190] Higher command officers could make proposals to training schools on which topics they believed should be covered at those schools.[191]

(Carlisle, PA: U.S. Army Heritage and Education Center, 2018 – 2019), 1.
[187]   Ibid.
[188]   Ibid.
[189]   Ibid., 7.
[190]   Ibid.
[191]   Ibid.

World War II continued on a trajectory of centralizing basic training. Learning from the mistakes of World War I, Chief of Staff General George Marshall and other senior leaders within the Army stated, "The War Department returned to a unit-based training plan, but this time made the Division Commander responsible for the facilitation of training at the regimental level and to certify its completion."[192] With increased power, the Division Commander was now able to oversee basic training to ensure quality control for the level and type of training each soldier received during basic training.

Even though basic training improved in quality during World War II, this did not translate into African-American soldiers being treated fairly. In fact, they still experienced discrimination at the outset of the conflict. Jim Crow laws were still in effect throughout America and the lynching of African-American men still frequently occurred. The country, however, was slowly changing. With the election of Franklin Roosevelt in 1932, the American government created a number of programs including Social Security and the Tennessee Valley Authority program which helped to inject new life into the American economy and, in turn, helped African-Americans secure a modicum of financial security.[193] President Roosevelt even made comments in support of civil rights, a move which was rare during this period in American history. This included speaking out against lynching and the poll tax, a reprehensible voting fee designed

---

[192]   Ibid., 8.

[193]   "Franklin Roosevelt," White House, accessed August 25, 2020, https://www.whitehouse.gov/about-the-white-house/presidents/franklin-d-roosevelt/.

to suppress the African-American vote. President Roosevelt also met with civil rights activists including Asa Randolph.[194] President Roosevelt's verbal support on specific areas of concern for the African-American community, while lacking in real substance, was at least a move in the right direction.

After World War II, African-American soldiers came home and were met with hostility by Whites. The old rules still applied. It did not matter that they served their country with distinction. Jim Crow laws remained imbedded in American society. African-Americans were still not granted the right to vote. Yet, something was different. In addition to Randolph's social activism, President Truman believed African-Americans who served in the U.S. military proved they were capable of being good, reliable soldiers. As a result of their military service, President Truman signed Executive Order 9981. Change was coming or so it appeared.

The transformation of the U.S. military into an institution which valued all soldiers would be a slow and arduous process. For example, basic training given to African-American soldiers underscored this point. Before the outbreak of the Korean War, African-American and White soldiers were still segregated in both the Army and Marine Corps, even though Executive Order 9981 abolished discrimination based on race, color or creed.[195]

---

[194] "Franklin D. Roosevelt: The American Franchise," University of Virginia Miller Center, accessed July 28, 2020, https://millercenter.org/president/fdroosevelt/the-american-franchise.

[195] Jeremy P. Maxwell, *Brotherhood in Combat: How African-Americans Found Equality in Korea and Vietnam* (Norman: University of Oklahoma Press, 2018), 71.

Despite the persistence of institutional racism within the U.S. military, the quality of basic training provided to all soldiers continued to improve. Like World War I and World War II, basic training was further modified to become more efficient during the Korean War era. The U.S. military decided centralized training of soldiers should take place at Army bases across the country.[196] To get soldiers prepared more quickly to be shipped out to duty stations faster, the U.S. Army cut basic training to eight weeks in 1948.[197] The Army created four "Training Divisions" to serve as training centers. At these training hubs, Unit Commanders oversaw advanced training for all soldiers.

Nonetheless, this new approach for preparing U.S. soldiers for combat did have a number of drawbacks. First, it "shifted an undue burden to a commander who did not, in most cases, have the resources to conduct the necessary training."[198] Second, it ignored "the readiness component, because units with large numbers of inexperienced, under-trained soldiers were not combat ready" at the start of the Korean War.[199] To make matters worse, all fighting units regardless of race received some weapons which were unreliable. Sub-optimal clothing at the beginning of the Korean War was given out to some White and African-American

---

[196]   Peter S. Kindsvatter, *American Soldiers: Ground Combat in the World Wars, Korea, and Vietnam* (Lawrence: University Press of Kansas, 2003), 17.

[197]   Conrad C. Crane, Michael E. Lynch, Shane P. Reilly, Jessica J. Sheets, *U.S. Army Heritage and Education Center, Learning the Lessons of Lethality: The Army's Cycle of Basic Combat Training, 1918 – 2019* (Carlisle, PA: U.S. Army Heritage and Education Center, 2018 – 2019), 1.

[198]   Ibid.

[199]   Ibid.

soldiers. Even so, this problem disproportionately affected African-American soldiers juxtaposed to their White counterparts.

Despite these problems, the U.S. military still provided basic training to their soldiers at the outset of the Korean War. Training camp for soldiers was made up of two different sections. The first part of training camp focused on marching, military courtesy, physical conditioning, rifle marksmanship, etc.[200] The second part of training camp featured more individualized training, concentrating on helping soldiers develop particular skills which were crucial to the war effort.[201] Within the first couple of weeks of basic training, soldiers were given a baseline of information and conditioning. Afterward, specialized training would be provided to soldiers based on their interest in particular areas and their scores on performance tests.

The objective of basic training camp was simple, "Teach recruits basic tactical, physical, and weapons skills while simultaneously instilling the discipline and behavioral norms necessary to succeed in combat."[202] As soldiers went through this process, a transformation took place where the "civilian minded recruit" was turned into a "reliable soldier programmed to respond according to expectations" which were determined by the U.S. military.[203] In effect, the U.S. military sought to destroy all elements of

---

[200]   Ibid.

[201]   Ibid.

[202]   Ibid.

[203]   Arthur J. Vidich and Maurice R. Stein, "The Dissolved Identity in Military Life," in *Identity and Anxiety: Survival of the Person in Mass Society*, ed. Maurice R. Stein, Arthur J. Vidich and David Manning White (Glencoe: Free Press, 1960), 496.

an individual's identity and rebuild a new person who took orders and carried out their duties required of them by the U.S. Armed Forces.

The tearing down process typically "lasted the first couple of weeks of a recruit's Army Basic Training or Marine Boot Camp."[204] Over a period of a few weeks, new recruits would be subjected to a gradual increase in stress and/or pain. It was part of a concerted effort to expose men to tolerable levels of stress.[205] The U.S. military believed intentionally increasing the stress level for soldiers would prepare them for battle.[206] If a soldier was wounded or if his friend was killed during a violent encounter with enemy combatants, the U.S. military hoped they would be conditioned to mentally stay focused and continue fighting.

Given the training all soldiers were required to go through before they headed to Korea, it would be safe to assume African-American soldiers would be valued just as much as White soldiers at the inception of the Korean War. This, however, was not the case. Some military decision-makers were hesitant to use African-American soldiers in combat because many were poorly educated.[207] The Far East command, for example, required African-American soldiers who did not complete the fifth-grade or who had scored poorly on aptitude tests to have more extensive training.[208] Indeed, African-American soldiers, even before they deployed

[204] Vidich and Stein, *Identity and Anxiety: Survival of the Person in Mass Society*, 18.
[205] Ibid.
[206] Ibid.
[207] Bernard Nalty, *Strength for the Fight: Black Americans in the Military* (New York: Free Press, 1986), 224-225.
[208] Nalty, *Strength for the Fight: Black Americans in the Military*, 224 – 225.

to Korea, had to prove their worth to the U.S. Armed Forces and show they were capable soldiers.

Nonetheless, African-American veterans from the Korean War suggest they were well trained in basic military skills, including the usage of weaponry and battlefield tactics. Soldiers who received individualized training, for example, learned how to administer medical care to injured soldiers, how to build bridges and how to remove bacteria and other toxins from water. Soldiers were also provided some tools to help them mentally survive the torments of war during their deployment in Korea.

At the most basic level, the training African-American soldiers received got them into shape physically. Curtis Morrow, a member of the 24th Infantry, recalled his basic training experience was rigorous. According to Morrow, basic training was tough because it "was all about physical education."[209] As he put it, "You got to exercise and running and jumping and climbing and pushups and then more pushups."[210] Morrow further stated soldiers had to "run, jog, maybe five miles or whatever, but mostly it was drilling, doing dismounted drills, which get to you. They were tiring and boring."[211] Basic training made Morrow more fit so he could withstand the physical demands of war in Korea. James Jenkins had a similar experience in basic training. According to Jenkins, "You had physical training. We had what they call PT (physical training) every day, exercise,

---

[209]   Curtis Morrow. Interviewed by Eliot Pope. Personal Interview. Chicago, Illinois, January 7th, 2015.
[210]   Ibid.
[211]   Ibid.

and strengthen your upper body, your lower body, and then marching. Every Wednesday, you went on a long march, forty, forty-five miles."[212]

After African-Americans finished basic training, they received Advanced Individual Training (AIT). Like White soldiers, African-American soldiers were often given a chance to request schools which would teach them specific skills like language, weapons, mechanical work, engineering and medicine. Ultimately, they would use these skills in the army.[213] James Lacy, for example, traveled to Gifu, Japan to train in weapons. Lacy recalled, "I wanted to go and the next school to open up was rifle repair, called Arm Artillery and I wanted to know what made my rifle operate and everything, and put my name up."[214] While Lacy was at rifle school, he was instructed on how to care for his weapon. As he put it, "I went to school and learned how to take weapons down and put them back together blindfolded. No light at all."[215]

For Morrow, weapons training was vital to his survival on the battlefield. Morrow was required to go to a class for weapons training and was also provided lessons on tactics to be employed in combat.[216] According to Morrow, the rifle the Army trained him with "was an eight-cartridge. I forget all of the specifications of it now, but it was a nine-pound. It would, if you put the bayonet on, probably come up to my chest. They teach you

[212]   Jesse Jenkins. Interviewed by Eliot Pope. Personal Interview. Crown Point, Indiana, February 18, 2015.
[213]   James Lacy. Interviewed by Eliot Pope. Personal Interview. Chicago, Illinois, January 20, 2015.
[214]   Ibid.
[215]   Ibid.
[216]   Ibid.

about the accuracy of it and so forth."[217] After Morrow was taught the basics about rifles, he and his fellow soldiers were taken to the rifle range to train by firing at targets.[218] At the rifle range, "They gave you live ammunition, and you use targets, oh man, for at least two weeks, just firing at bulls-eye targets."[219] Through this training, Morrow became skilled at firing a rifle. Eventually, he qualified as a sharpshooter.

The training African-American soldiers received changed them both physically and mentally. After surviving boot camp, soldiers became more resilient. Morrow reported, "They are making you tough because they are going to make you prove you are worthy of being there. That is the philosophy, I guess, or psychology behind the whole thing."[220] This mental toughness which was bred into soldiers at basic training gave them an edge when they went into combat zones. As Morrow put it, "Hell, I am going to do it or die trying."[221] His scrappy attitude helped to build his resilience. He said, "People can say things or try to do things to try to discourage you, but F them. [*laughs*] I'm cleaning it up, right?"[222] This never give up attitude kept Morrow alive when he went to war. Basic training gave African-American soldiers a fearless mentality, helping them fight against North Korean and Chinese enemy combatants and racist White soldiers.

---

[217] Ibid.
[218] Ibid.
[219] Ibid.
[220] Curtis Morrow. Interviewed by Eliot Pope. Personal Interview. Chicago, Illinois, January 7th, 2015.
[221] Ibid.
[222] Ibid.

Racist sentiments were more prevalent among Whites from certain regions in America. Lacy, a member of the 24th, revealed racism toward African-American soldiers came largely from White soldiers from the South. According to Lacy, "Some of the guys, the officers, were like, they were from down South. They were kind of rough with the colored soldiers."[223] Lacy observed southern soldiers disrespected African-American soldiers. By contrast, he witnessed White soldiers from New York and New Jersey put pressure on southern Whites to treat African-American soldiers with respect. As Lacy said, "They kept them in line."[224] Lacy's remarks suggest southern and northern soldiers diverged on how African-American soldiers should be treated. On the one hand, some southern soldiers wanted to ensure African-American soldiers remained in a subservient position within the U.S. military. Some northern soldiers, on the other hand, lobbied for African-American soldiers to be treated with dignity. In the end, Lacy asserted northern soldiers protected African-American soldiers from discriminatory practices waged against them by their southern counterparts.

Lacy's experience notwithstanding, a White soldier willing to intervene on behalf of African-American soldiers remained a relative rarity. In some cases, African-American soldiers were forced to defend themselves against racist White soldiers. William Love, a Korean War veteran, experienced racism while he was at a U.S. base. After Love took an apti-

---

[223] James Lacy. Interviewed by Eliot Pope. Personal Interview. Chicago, Illinois, January 20, 2015.
[224] Ibid.

tude test, he qualified to do twelve or thirteen jobs in the U.S. military.[225] Love elected to be a coordinator/dispatcher of Army trucks. During his training, Love was obligated to drive with a White man in his vehicle. While he was driving the truck, he reported he and his partner "would slap each other every day" as they drove the truck during training.[226] Later, Love revealed when he was away from the man, "He would be looking for me."[227]

Some African-American soldiers rationalized the racism they encountered at U.S. Army bases during the Korean War era. Before Morrow described the racism he received during basic training, he indicated, "Most of the guys you got to deal with, they were not that way."[228] Morrow expressed the majority of the White soldiers he knew treated him fairly and with respect. In cases where he did encounter racism during basic training, he said, "People do not like you because you are African-American. You ask them why, they could not tell you."[229] He added, "There is always a few assholes just everywhere you go."[230] By framing the prejudice he experienced as part of a larger trend within American society, Morrow reasoned the racism he experienced as an issue he had to manage to successfully complete basic training.

---

[225] William Love. Interviewed by Eliot Pope. Personal Interview. Chicago, Illinois, October 29, 2014.
[226] Ibid.
[227] Ibid.
[228] Curtis Morrow. Interviewed by Eliot Pope. Personal Interview. Chicago, Illinois, January 7th, 2015.
[229] Ibid.
[230] Ibid.

In addition to Morrow's rationalization of racism he faced as a part of life, he also reframed the racism he endured during basic training as an incentive to get stronger. As he put it, "I had to deal with it. Actually, on base, it was great. It was Black hate. I ate it up, man. I liked it."[231] In other words, Morrow used the racism he encountered during basic training to make him more resilient. His statement indicates he weathered a significant amount of racism during his basic training. Nevertheless, he refused to let the prejudice he confronted stop him from training to be the best soldier he could be. His ability to recycle the bigotry he experienced and transform it into reusable energy was remarkable. Morrow's unique coping mechanism for managing racism encouraged him to constantly look for ways to improve as a soldier. Beyond that, it reveals his mental fortitude. Hence, for some African-American soldiers, training hard to become a competent soldier became a form of redemption against racial hostility they experienced during basic training.

While Morrow did face discrimination from other White soldiers, he argued racist officers were the exception rather than the rule. According to Morrow, "I do not recall getting any racism from the officers, because my officer, he was actually from the North. He was a straight dude."[232] Morrow's account suggests he believed prejudice against African-Americans soldiers appeared unevenly across the U.S. military.

---

[231] Ibid.
[232] Ibid.

One explanation for why White enlisted men possibly harbored more racism is because they viewed African-American soldiers as a potential threat. By contrast, African-American soldiers were nearly universally of a different rank and authority than White officers and therefore unavailable as competitors. Finally, most White officers were better educated than White enlisted men and, consequently, viewed African-American soldiers through an empathic lens. Clearly, rank and region played a defining role in whether or not White soldiers were overtly racist.

Additionally, some African-American Korean War veterans highlighted subtle forms of racism which affected their experiences. For example, Homer Franklin, an African-American soldier who served in the Korean War, details encountering an undercurrent of racism from his commanding officer. Franklin revealed his commanding officer was a kind, understanding southern gentleman from Tennessee. He was a "very, very unusual Southerner."[233] He treated African-American men whom he commanded with guarded respect. Despite this, Franklin says his commanding officer made sure to establish a delineation between himself as a "White governing, managing, commanding officer and the rest of us as enlisted African-American men."[234] Franklin's statement exposes the underlying bias his commanding officer had against African-American soldiers. The barrier the commanding officer erected between himself

---

[233] Homer Franklin. Interviewed by Eliot Pope. Personal Interview. Chicago, Illinois, November 28, 2014.

[234] Ibid.

and his soldiers suggest racial tensions lurking beneath the surface may have affected the relationship.

Nevertheless, African-American soldiers were more prepared at the outset of the Korea War than previous conflicts they participated in. They were physically conditioned to meet the demands of the Korean War. Pushups, pull-ups, squats and marching on a daily basis strengthened their bodies. The instruction they received on how to read a map, how to use a gun and bayonet, and how to track enemy soldiers indicates they were prepared for war. They were provided with some of the tools to succeed on the battlefield. With better training, came more responsibility. Unlike in World War I where they were pushed to the margins of the U.S. military, dismissed as little more than small, inconsequential cogs within the vast organizational structure of the U.S. Armed Forces, African-American soldiers during the Korean War would frequently engage in armed combat. Ensign Jesse Brown flying a state-of-the-art Navy airplane proves this point. African-American soldiers were not mere pawns in the game. They now mattered. In spite of the various forms of racial oppression they endured, African-American soldiers were now granted a chance to prove their manhood on the battlefields of Korea.

CHAPTER 3
Combat

"I have been trying to get a chance to write you for the last three days but without much success. I would like to write you every night. I love to tell you that I love and adore you, and, although I never quite succeeded in getting it across, I like to try and tell you how much I care and how much you really mean to me. So you see, my darling, not only do I like to hear you tell me that you love me but I like telling you also that you're the sweetest woman in the world. I love you, Angel, and I want you to know that my heart belongs to you." – Ensign Jesse Brown to Daisy, December 3rd, 1950[235]

Ensign Jesse Brown's letter to Daisy, his high school sweetheart and confidant, revealed how important she was to him. She was his lover, friend and pseudo-therapist all rolled into one. Daisy gave Brown faith. She was his rock, never wavering and always committed. Letters he wrote to Daisy were like safety valves. They let him blow off some steam, to

---

[235]   Theodore Taylor, *The Flight of Jesse Leroy Brown*, (Annapolis: Naval Institute Press, 2007), 268.

dream of one day waking up next to his beautiful wife in his arms. Escapism at its finest. Daisy gave Brown hope a better day was around the corner if he could just hold on. Above all, she motivated him to fight on with honor and dignity. After Brown finished his letter, he went to sleep.

When Brown woke the next morning, he was met with coldness which struck all the way to his bones and gave him chills which ran down his spine. He snapped into action. He threw on his long underwear, coveralls, a sweater, fleece-lined boots and gloves and made his way to the mess area where he picked up his usual coffee. Coffee gave him a jolt, a spark of energy. While he was in the mess area, Brown's best friend, Lee Nelson, came over to Brown and said, "It's ugly out there."[236]

Brown asked Nelson, "Any ack-ack antiaircraft fire?"[237]

Nelson replied, "The usual around Chosin. Small arms."[238] Nelson had already been baptized by the cold, blustery wind and small arms fire earlier in the day when he flew right below the Manchurian border, attacking enemy positions which were mobilizing on the northwest shore of Korea.[239]

Brown replied, "Man, am I sleepy. I was up late writing to Daisy."[240]

Nelson laughed. "You'll wake up once you get on deck. It's cold, Brown. Same as yesterday."[241]

---

[236] Taylor, *The Flight of Jesse Leroy Brown*, 2.
[237] Ibid.
[238] Ibid.
[239] Ibid.
[240] Ibid.
[241] Ibid.

Brown took the last few sips of his coffee and said briskly, "Gotta go."[242]

Brown hopped into his Vought F4U Corsair, one of six airplanes which were part of the Iroquois Flight Group. The Corsair was one ruthless airplane. It was like a fire-breathing dragon with a chip on its shoulder. It was fast, with the ability to reach speeds of over four hundred miles per hour. It could generate over two thousand horsepower on take off and pump one hundred and fifty rounds into enemy targets from its six .50 caliber machine guns in roughly two seconds.[243]

Brown took off from aircraft carrier *Leyte* (CV 33) on December 4th, 1950. Once airborne, the six airplanes of the Iroquois squadron climbed and headed to the vicinity of Chosin, about one hundred miles away. Brown's mission provided air support for U.S. Marines and soldiers who were under attack by Chinese soldiers. His squadron of six Corsairs flew over the North Korean coastline at just over one thousand feet above the hostile terrain. The planes then dropped to around five hundred feet to locate targets after they crossed the coastline just north of Hungnam. Flying on the west side of Chosin, they entered the Chosin reservoir, a beautiful, serene body of water which had majestic pine trees lining its shores. Snow covered the area.[244]

Beneath the snow lay something more sinister. Chinese soldiers dressed in white snowsuits laid in the snow. Their mission was simple –

---

[242] Ibid.
[243] Ibid., 4.
[244] Ibid.

shot enemy aircraft that came within their range of fire. They did not have big, powerful, fancy anti-aircraft guns which could easily bring down a plane. They had to rely on ingenuity. As American attack planes entered their air space, Chinese soldiers pointed their guns into the air and fired a barrage of bullets into the sky. Sometimes Chinese soldiers got lucky and hit an American warplane. Brown's aircraft fell victim to a bullet fired by one of the Chinese soldiers hidden in the snow.[245]

Brown yelled out, "I have been hit. I am losing fuel pressure."[246]

Koenig, one of the other Navy pilots who were a part of the Iroquois group at 2:40 p.m., told him, "You are dumping fuel!"[247]

Brown calmly said, "This is Iroquois 1-3, I am losing fuel pressure. I have to put it down."[248]

Koenig radioed, "Mayday, Mayday," letting the flight deck know one of their own aircraft was in trouble.[249]

Brown prepped his airplane for a crash landing. He abruptly dropped his flaps. He got rid of his fuel and jettisoned the belly tank and rockets attached to the underbelly of his Corsair. Meanwhile, Lieutenant Tom Hudner, his wingman, went over the emergency checklist with him. Hudner knew Brown was in bad shape, but did not show it. He said calmly, "Lock your harness, open your canopy and lock it."[250]

---

[245] Ibid., 4 – 5.
[246] Ibid., 2.
[247] Ibid., 4-5.
[248] Ibid.
[249] Ibid.
[250] Ibid., 5.

Being a good, devoted wingman, Hudner followed Brown down for his inevitable crash landing. "Two hundred feet! One hundred feet! Hold it steady — fifty feet — here you go!"[251] The plane was struggling to stay in the air as if it was gasping for its last breath. Then, the plane abruptly dropped the last twenty-five feet, smashing into a mountain covered with snow. Propeller blades and chunks of the plane flew everywhere. The engine detached from the airplane. The tail of Brown's aircraft slammed into the ground.[252] The smell of fuel filled the air.

Brown's airplane crashed into a bowl-shaped valley fifteen miles behind enemy lines at around 3 p.m. It was a hard crash, but he survived. Brown's left knee, however, got trapped in the rubble. He was stuck like a bug in a Venus flytrap. Moments later Hudner made a heroic landing next to Brown's aircraft. With no tools to remove Brown's leg from the wreckage, Hudner struggled to free Brown. As Hudner pushed and pulled, it became clear resistance was futile. Brown started to get tired. The agonizing pain he felt in his leg began to fade. He then slipped into unconsciousness and died.[253]

The stakes were high for African-Americans during the Korean War. Unlike during World War II, where only a select few African-Americans saw combat, many African-Americans would be given a chance to fight during the Korean War. This provided a unique opportunity for them.

---

[251] Ibid., 5-6.

[252] Ibid.

[253] Adam Makos, *Devotion: An Epic Story of Heroism, Friendship, and Sacrifice*, (New York: Ballantine Books, 2017), 354 – 355.

If they served their country during a time of war, then perhaps African-Americans at home would be given greater freedom. Some even believed perhaps America would reevaluate its commitment to Jim Crow and remove it once and for all from American society. Still others believed it would afford them a chance to prove their manhood.

During battle, African-American soldiers were not morally righteous heroes, although there were instances where they did display a high level of piety. They were not evil, diabolical murderers, though there were instances where they did display a degree of uncanny cruelty. African-American soldiers were complicated. Despite the racism they endured and the unique challenges they faced, African-American soldiers served their country with dignity and honor. Taking into account the constant assaults on their character, the battle-hardened North Korean and Chinese soldiers they faced and the freezing temperatures they endured, African-American soldiers revealed their humanity, ruthlessness and perseverance.

The Korean War began on June 25th, 1950. North Korean soldiers crossed the 38th parallel and headed for Seoul, the capital of South Korea. As an ally to South Korea, the United States immediately sent troops to defend the country. President Truman viewed the attack on South Korea by North Korea as a clear and present danger to democracy on the Korean peninsula. In order to prevent the spread of communism, President Truman believed U.S. troops and soldiers from the North Atlantic Treaty Organization (NATO) must be deployed to push the Korean People's Army (KPA) back into North Korean territory.

The first African-American soldier set foot on South Korean soil on July 12th, 1950.[254] Among the six million eight hundred thousand American men and women who served in the U.S. military during the Korean War, 339,400 were of African-American descent.[255] When African-American soldiers arrived in Korea, they entered a new world filled with novel sights, smells and people. They saw vast stretches of supply trucks and tents. They saw battle-hardened veterans. They saw the wounded and dead. Once settled, African-American soldiers took up their wartime duties. Some worked in medical units while others worked on supply lines. Some African-American soldiers helped to construct bridges and others helped to keep the supply lines up and running. Many, of course, engaged in combat with the enemy.

When African-American soldiers arrived on the Korean peninsula in 1950, they entered a country approximately six hundred miles long and one hundred and twenty miles from coast to coast. Roughly the size of Utah and with a landmass of 84,565 square miles, Korea was a relatively small country.[256] Sprinkled with mountain ranges, hills, hollows

---

[254] William T. Bowers, William M. Hammond, and George L. MacGarrigle, *Black Soldier, White Army: The 24th Infantry Regiment in Korea* (Washington: Center of Military History, 1996), 82.

[255] United States, U.S. Department of Veterans Affairs, *U.S. Department of Veterans Affairs: Data on Veterans of The Korean War – Assistant Secretary for Planning and Analysis Office of Program and Data Analyses* (Washington, D.C.: U.S. Department of Veterans Affairs, 2000), 1.

[256] "The Geography of the Koreas," Asia Society, accessed on June 22, 2020, https://asiasociety.org/education/geography-koreas.

and valleys, terrain on the Korean peninsula was treacherous.[257] Nestled in between the hills and mountains were rice paddies, rivers and shallow streams. The rice paddies, often located near rivers and streams, gave off a pungent smell. As one Korean War veteran put it, if you were on patrol and fell in, "It was pretty gross. You could not wait to get back to wash up."[258] Due to the putrid smells coming from the rivers and rice paddies, patrols were almost unbearable.

Additionally, the steep mountains posed a physical challenge for many soldiers. Pulling heavy equipment, including machine guns, tents, food rations and sleeping bags, up hills and mountains was exhausting. As the soldiers moved up and down the mountains and hills, they encountered a range of different types of trees depending upon where they were located in Korea. In North Korea, coniferous forests filled with fir, spruce, larch, walnut and birch trees greeted soldiers. Soldiers discovered broad-leaved deciduous trees in the cool temperate forests which were located towards the middle of Korea. Oak, ash and pine trees were often found here. In South Korea, which is shaped similar to a human foot, a mixture of deciduous and coniferous forests packed with oak trees welcomed soldiers.[259]

Trees and other foliage on the hills and mountains of Korea gave soldiers a number of advantages. The trees provided protective cover,

---

[257] "Terrain," filmed 2021, Government of Canada video, 1:23. https://www.veterans.gc.ca/eng/remembrance/history/korean-war/land-morning-calm/conditions/terrain.

[258] Ibid.

[259] "Forestry in Korea," World Forestry Center, accessed on June 22nd, 2020, https://www.worldforestry.org/wp-content/uploads/2015/11/korea_s.lee.pdf.

shielding them from gunfire and mortar shells which rained down from the sky. Soldiers could use the vegetation as camouflage, blending in with the environment, hiding them from enemy combatants. They could climb trees and use them to set up sniper nests. From this vantage point, snipers could easily target and then subsequently kill enemy combatants. When temperatures got cold, soldiers could use branches and bark from trees to make small fires which kept them warm. If it got windy, trees, shrubs and bushes slowed down the strong winds. The terrain the Korean War was fought on was tough, but African-American soldiers learned how to survive within it.

Korea's unique climate also affected African-American soldiers' ability to wage war. Spring in Korea, which lasts from mid-March until May, is initially cold but overtime becomes milder. Summer, on the other hand, typically is hot and humid. Large amounts of rain usually cause flooding and landslides during this season. Meanwhile, fall in Korea is fairly mild.[260] The trees turn colors. The air becomes crisp. As winter approaches, Korea becomes cold and cloudy. The days are shorter. Bitter cold engulfs the Korean peninsula. Mountainous areas freeze. It was during this season the weather became a formidable adversary.

When African-American soldiers arrived in Korea in 1951, they would become familiarized with this powerful foe. When winter hit African-American soldiers, they were in for a rude awakening.[261] Some got

---

[260] "Climate – South Korea," Climates to Travel, accessed on June 23, 2020, https://www.climatestotravel.com/climate/south-korea.

[261] Ibid.

frostbite and others died of hypothermia. Frigid temperatures posed a significant threat to all soldiers stationed in Korea, but African-American soldiers were especially vulnerable to the weather given their inadequate clothing and sleeping quarters.

The weather conditions could have been mitigated with proper equipment. Warm jackets, gloves, and hats could have shielded African-Americans from the harsh temperatures. Nevertheless, institutionalized racism contributed to the challenges cold weather posed for African-American soldiers. As with weaponry, the U.S. military did not provide African-American soldiers with adequate equipment to face the cold weather. Instead, they had to make do with used winter gear which was insufficient and unreliable. According to William Bowers, William Hammond, and George MacGarrigle, the 24th Infantry was given the opportunity to choose "one fur or pile-lined garment, be it a field jacket, cap, or gloves."[262] As a result of these restrictions, African-American soldiers were forced to choose what extremities they would cover and which ones they would leave exposed to the weather. The insufficient supplies increased the likelihood African-American soldiers would suffer injury or die from the frigid temperatures. Consequently, a number of African-American soldiers perished due to hypothermia and many more got frostbite.[263]

---

[262]   William T. Bowers, William M. Hammond, and George L. MacGarrigle, *Black Soldier, White Army: The 24th Infantry Regiment in Korea* (Washington D.C.: Center of Military History, 1996), 82.

[263]   Bowers, Hammond and MacGarrigle, *Black Soldier, White Army: The 24th Infantry Regiment in Korea*, 82.

Since the U.S. military at the beginning of the Korean War suffered from equipment shortages, it is safe to assume a number of White soldiers were not given adequate clothing to combat the frigid temperatures they faced. As a result, some White soldiers got frostbite on their legs, feet, hands, arms and face. Meanwhile, other White soldiers died from being exposed for too long to the extreme cold. Even so, a disproportionate number of White soldiers, however, were not forced to choose which extremities to cover, but were issued an adequate supply of cold weather gear. Thus, frigid temperatures in conjunction with institutionalized racism posed a serious threat to African-American soldiers in Korea.

The 24th's arrival in Korea illustrates the fatal potential of the cold. When Curtis Morrow landed at Inchon, he, along with other members of the 24th, witnessed "frozen bodies of American soldiers being sent back" on the backs of trucks.[264] African-American troops and some White soldiers were dying not only from bullets and shrapnel, but also from sub-zero temperatures. Morrow's original encounter foreshadowed the cold, blustery conditions he would face himself. Jesse Jenkins suggested, "It got forty below in the woods over there."[265] James Lacy indicated it became "as cold as fifty degrees" below zero.[266] Due to the lower temperatures, everything around the soldiers froze. As Morrow noted, "The food is frozen. Everything is frozen. You eat snow for water. The water is frozen,

---

[264] Curtis Morrow. Interviewed by Eliot Pope. Personal Interview. Chicago, Illinois, January 7th, 2015.

[265] Jesse Jenkins. Interviewed by Eliot Pope. Personal Interview. Crown Point, Indiana, February 18, 2015.

[266] James Lacy. Interviewed by Eliot Pope. Personal Interview. Chicago, Illinois, January 20, 2015.

man. Everything is frozen. You take a leak. It's frozen before it hit the . . ." Morrow laughed before continuing, "Everything is frozen. Your breath. If you've got a mustache, that froze."[267] To make matters worse, the U.S. military did not give African-American soldiers the proper tools to fight off the cold temperatures. As Lacy put it, "We did not have the appropriate equipment. We did not have nothing that was proper."[268]

To survive the cold temperatures, African-American soldiers had to develop a variety of different methods to stay warm. Lacy, for example, describes how he handled the discomfort and danger of wet feet after marching for long hours. To ensure he had a dry pair of socks to wear the next day, and thereby avoid immersion (trench) foot, Lacy took off his socks and put them in his armpits each night.[269] Sleeping bags presented another challenge to both staying warm and staying alive. Using sleeping bags came with risk because Chinese and North Korean soldiers often attacked at night.[270] According to one African-American veteran, in some instances the zipper on sleeping bags would freeze from a soldier's vapor he exhaled.[271] Because Chinese and North Korean forces typically attacked at night, they could "catch you in a sleeping bag" and kill you.[272] In other words, the sleeping bag could entrap soldiers, making it difficult for them to fight back. To solve this problem, some African-American soldiers put

---

[267] Curtis Morrow. Interviewed by Eliot Pope. Personal Interview. Chicago, Illinois, January 7th, 2015.
[268] James Lacy. Interviewed by Eliot Pope. Personal Interview. Chicago, Illinois, January 20, 2015.
[269] Ibid.
[270] Ibid.,
[271] Ibid.,
[272] Ibid.,

their sleeping bags only up to their waist.[273] Using only half of the bag gave soldiers a chance to warm their lower body while also giving them enough mobility to defend themselves if they were attacked. In response to these disadvantages, however, many soldiers avoided using their sleeping bags.

Due to the dilemma between staying warm while also remaining mobile enough to fight, soldiers like Morrow did not get much sleep while they were on the frontlines. In the face of extremely low temperatures and inadequate shelter, they risked freezing to death if they fell asleep for too long. Movement was key. As Morrow put it, "Everything is frozen, so you cannot stop moving. You will freeze. If you lay down and go to sleep, you will never wake up."[274] One solution was teamwork. According to Morrow, "One guy [would be] asleep on a cat nap while the other one stays awake so you can wake him up."[275] Additionally, soldiers sometimes learned how to sleepwalk. Morrow stated, "If you feel safe enough, you can put your hand on the guys in front of you and nod off."[276] Nevertheless, nodding off while marching was problematic in some ways. Soldiers who marched while drowsing off could hardly pay attention to the enemy or their environment. A primary concern was slipping through the ice of a rice paddy and getting soaked.[277] As Morrow put it, "If it is not completely frozen, if you break through the ice of the rice paddy, of the water which was once

---

[273] Ibid.,
[274] Curtis Morrow. Interviewed by Eliot Pope. Personal Interview. Chicago, Illinois, January 7th, 2015.
[275] Ibid.
[276] Ibid.
[277] Ibid.

there, you can get soaked. Then you will get frozen. You could freeze."[278] African-American soldiers used various methods to carry on with their duties in spite of the frigid temperatures they were subjected to. Morrow took naps as he marched with his fellow soldiers. As Morrow marched with other soldiers, he learned how to doze off for a few minutes at a time. In doing so, Morrow generated heat which kept him warm while also reenergizing himself by getting some sleep.

Despite the institutional racism African-American soldiers faced, their creativity in addressing the cold, frigid temperatures was remarkable. Their dogged determination ensured many of them would, in fact, survive. It is this quality which many African-American soldiers displayed which suggests they were more than capable of meeting and exceeding the demands placed on them during the Korean War. Like a prizefighter with one arm tied behind his back who still prevails in a boxing match, many African-American soldiers overcame a lack of cold weather equipment to combat freezing temperatures to serve their country honorably.

Just as the frigid temperatures posed a serious threat to the health and well-being of African-American soldiers, North Korean and Chinese soldiers proved to be worthy adversaries on the battlefield. In fact, many African-American soldiers respected North Korean and Chinese soldiers and viewed them as tough, brutal and intelligent fighters. These qualities were on display throughout the Korean War as African-American soldiers engaged in armed combat. North Korean soldiers would attack the front

---

[278]   Ibid.

of a U.S. military position. Poking and probing the frontlines of the U.S. military, the North Korean army's versatility helped them exploit weak points which helped them fight effectively against U.S. Armed Forces. If the attack did not work, North Korean soldiers would spread out and attack from the flanks.[279]

Chinese and North Korean strategies were not the only way to measure their effectiveness against the U.S. military. The sheer will and determination of North Korean and Chinese soldiers as they engaged U.S. soldiers forced the U.S. military to take them seriously. Often Chinese soldiers did not have helmets or protection against shrapnel. However, they made up for lack of equipment with unbridled determination to kill as many U.S. and NATO soldiers as possible. They were ruthless fighters.[280]

One African-American soldier described how North Korean soldiers would come "right into your foxhole, try and shoot you or stab you or bite you if they did not have a weapon. Just fanatical as hell."[281] North Koreans would use any weapon at their disposal to kill U.S. soldiers. They mutilated dead bodies of U.S. and NATO soldiers. They shot and killed prisoners indiscriminately.[282] Some African-American soldiers like Isaac Mercer, for example, viewed North Korean soldiers as vicious, tough adversar-

---

[279] Lyle Rishell, *With a Black Platoon in Combat* (College Station: Texas A&M University Press, 1993), 39.

[280] Vickie Spring, *Voices Almost Lost: Korea The Forgotten War* (Bloomington: Authorhouse Press, 2011), 107.

[281] Lyle Rishell, *With a Black Platoon in Combat* (College Station: Texas A&M University Press, 1993), 39.

[282] Michael Green, *Black Yanks in the Pacific: Race in the Making of American Military Empire after World War II* (Ithaca: Cornell University Press, 2010), 133.

ies.[283] Other African-American soldiers like Jesse Jenkins viewed them in a more positive light. He thought they were "tremendous fighters."[284] While sentiments ranged from North Korean and Chinese soldiers being resilient to being fanatical and ruthless, all accounts indicated they were competent soldiers, committed to winning at all cost.

The mind games North Korean and Chinese soldiers used against African-American soldiers were cruel yet effective techniques designed to break their spirits. These unethical stratagems made all American soldiers, including African-American soldiers, more susceptible to having mental breakdowns which would render them useless as soldiers. Roy Dell Johnson recalled North Korean and Chinese soldiers engaged in psychological warfare against African-American soldiers by mutilating some of the bodies of the dead.[285] According to Johnson, who struggled to find a way to express the atrocity, "You could, you run up GS [general support] and, you know, men are dead and their testicles are in their mouths. So, what I was saying is they worked on your brain, man, you know?"[286] North Korean and Chinese soldiers' usage of psychological warfare against African-American soldiers left deep scars on their psyches.

---

[283]   Isaac Mercer. Interviewed by Mark DePue. Personal Interview. Dixon, Illinois, December 29, 2010. James Lacy. Interviewed by Eliot Pope. Personal Interview. Chicago, Illinois, January 20, 2015. Lacy viewed Chinese fighters as fierce fighters that attacked American positions in large numbers. Lacy stated that his religion helped him cope with the massive attacks. At the request of other soldiers, he recited, "Hail Mary, full of grace, the Lord is with thee" as bombs rained down on him and his fellow soldiers. Lacy and other soldiers chanted the Hail Mary prayer in unison until the bombing subsided.

[284]   Jesse Jenkins. Interviewed by Eliot Pope. Personal Interview. Crown Point, Indiana, February 18, 2015.

[285]   Roy Dell Johnson. Interviewed by Eliot Pope. Personal Interview. Arlington, Texas, March 2, 2015.

[286]   Ibid.

North Korean and Chinese soldiers' intelligence was highlighted not only through the psychological violence they waged against American troops, but also through tactics they used on the battlefield. Clarence Senor, an African-American Korean War veteran, recalled traveling on a boat in North Korea and observing North Korean soldiers try to hit U.S. ships with boats rigged with explosives.[287] If these boats made contact with American ships, they caused significant damage, killing men and destroying supplies. [288]

Furthermore, North Korean and Chinese armies used asymmetrical warfare to strike American troops when they least expected it. For instance, the NKPA (North Korean Peoples' Army) used children to kill American soldiers. In one instance, a young Korean boy ran up to a military vehicle, yelled 'GI!' and then dropped two hand grenades, killing everyone inside the vehicle.[289] Using children to kill American soldiers was ruthless but shrewd. Because they are usually viewed as nonthreatening, the NKPA knew children could get close to U.S. soldiers and kill them.

The NKPA took advantage of rules of engagement established during the Geneva Convention of 1949, leaving American soldiers open for potential attacks. The Geneva Convention was established to ensure civilians were not hurt during armed conflict between two opposing armies. According to Article four, "Persons protected by the Convention are those

---

[287] Clarence Senor. Interviewed by Mark DePue. Springfield, Illinois, November 5, 2008.
[288] Ibid.
[289] Michael Green, *Black Yanks in the Pacific: Race in the Making of American Military Empire after World War II* (Ithaca: Cornell University Press, 2010), 133.

who, at a given moment and in any manner whatsoever, find themselves, in case of a conflict or occupation, in the hands of a Party to the conflict or Occupying Power of which they are not nationals."[290] Since North Korean children were considered civilians under the Geneva Conventions, children were protected from hostilities from U.S. Armed Forces. NKPA's usage of children gave them an unfair advantage during armed combat with the U.S. military.[291]

When African-American soldiers arrived in Korea at the outset of the Korean War in 1950, the U.S. military was still largely segregated, even though it was moving gradually toward integration following Executive Order 9981. Some branches of the U.S. military and certain individual combat units were integrated, while other parts of the U.S. Armed Forces resisted the change. The integration of African-American and White soldiers in the U.S. military was done in an inconsistent, illogical manner.[292] Consequently, the U.S. military's haphazard integration policy created uncertainty for African-American soldiers, White soldiers and U.S. military commanders. The lack of sensitivity applied to the process of integrating the U.S. military created a boiling broth of racism which threatened to destabilize the U.S. Armed Forces.

Because the U.S. military's commitment to desegregating the armed forces was not a priority, many African-Americans faced some form of

---

[290] "Geneva Convention Article 4, 1949," International Committee of the Red Cross, accessed on March 15, 2016, 36. https://www.icrc.org/applic/ihl/ihl.nsf/ART/365-570008?OpenDocument.

[291] *Geneva Convention Article 4*, 36.

[292] Kimberley Phillips, *War! What Is It Good For?* (Chapel Hill: The University of North Carolina Press, 2012), 145.

racism while stationed in Korea during the war. Racism can be broken into three types: physical racism, institutionalized racism, and a subtle, passive-aggressive form of racism. Charles Armstrong, one of the first African-American commanders of an integrated company, highlights the struggle African-American soldiers faced.[293] Armstrong indicated he felt marginalized as an officer because he was subject to institution-alized racism in the U.S. military during the Korean War. As Armstrong put it, "I knew it was a losing battle, but I wanted to serve my country. So few of us were commissioned officers, people were looking to me to be successful. I felt it was my obligation to fight. I thought I would benefit, but I did not."[294] Even though he achieved a fairly high rank within the U.S. military, he discovered his position in the U.S. Armed Forces did not shield him from racism.

On a broader level, institutional racism also hurt the effectiveness of African-American soldiers. William Bowers, William Hammond, and George MacGarrigle argue institutional racism, among other factors, limited the military effectiveness of the 24th.[295] According to the authors, the unit failed because of antiquated equipment, incompetent and/or inexperience at all levels, problems with leadership, high casualty rates among key personnel and the lack of solidarity within some units.[296]

---

[293] Phillips, *War! What Is It Good For?*, 145.

[294] Ibid.

[295] William T. Bowers, William M. Hammond, and George L. MacGarrigle, *Black Soldier, White Army: The 24th Infantry Regiment in Korea* (Washington D.C.: Center of Military History, 1996), 267.

[296] Bowers, Hammond and MacGarrigle, *Black Soldier, White Army: The 24th Infantry Regiment in Korea*, 267.

The 24th's poor experience during the war was determined by the lack of quality gear and leadership they received compared to all-White infantry units. Simply put, systemic issues embedded within the U.S. military, not the quality of training they received during basic training, were key factors in the 24th's poor performance on the battlefields in Korea.[297]

Lack of quality weapons given to African-American soldiers put them at a distinct disadvantage during the Korean War. The 24th, for example, received inferior World War II-vintage weapons and communications equipment.[298] Because the weapons were old and outdated, they sometimes broke. [299] Conversely, White units often received newer equipment. After 1945, the U.S. government shifted its attention away from maintaining the military since the country did not face any imminent threats.[300] The logic used to disseminate weapons to soldiers was racist. Since African-American soldiers were deemed as lower quality than White soldiers, the U.S. military decided to allocate most old weaponry to African-American soldiers. Inversely, White soldiers, deemed higher quality than African-American soldiers, usually were given newer weapons because they were perceived to be worthy of getting only the best. While there were many exceptions to this rule, the disproportionate number of newer weapons handed out to all-White combat units juxta-

---

[297]   Ibid.

[298]   Lyle Rishell, *With a Black Platoon in Combat* (College Station: Texas A&M University Press, 1993), 40.

[299]   Rishell, *With a Black Platoon in Combat*, 40.

[300]   William T. Bowers, William M. Hammond, and George L. MacGarrigle, *Black Soldier, White Army: The 24th Infantry Regiment in Korea* (Washington D.C.: Center of Military History, 1996), 65.

posed to African-American fighting units suggests the U.S. military was creating the circumstances for the unit to fail.

James Williams, a machine gunner for the 24th and 27th Infantries, observed in the 24th the military-issued "boots and things were used. You did not get nothing new."[301] Old and unreliable supplies given to African-American soldiers often broke down while they were out on the frontlines fighting. Williams further stated, "We had the World War II equipment. It broke down."[302] He observed machine guns used in African-American regiments were less reliable than those used in White regiments. As he explained, "We did not ever get no new barrels, see? In a machine gun, you can burn the barrel out. You can fire it until the barrel turns cherry red. When it is like that you done burned it out."[303] Williams added, "In the middle of the fire fight, you got to change this barrel, put another barrel in, and start back to work again."[304] The poor quality of equipment provided to the 24th sent a powerful message to its African-American soldiers: the U.S. military did not value their contributions to the war effort in Korea.

In contrast, many White soldiers were outfitted with new gear and weapons. Indeed, when Williams went to the 27th, he saw the difference in stark contrast.[305] He reported the 27th, which was a desegregated unit during the war "got brand new barrels" for their machine guns which did

---

301   James Williams. Interviewed by Eliot Pope. Personal Interview. Chicago, Illinois, January 12, 2015.
302   Ibid.
303   Ibid.
304   Ibid.
305   Ibid.

not break down.[306] The decision to issue the 27th new equipment while restricting the 24th to old equipment was racially motivated. Ultimately, this form of institutional racism created conditions for the 24th to fail by ill-equipping it for combat and by demoralizing it.

Not only were African-American soldiers often ill-equipped to fight against both the frigid temperatures and battle-hardened North Korean and Chinese soldiers, but their units were required to fight for longer periods of time than White units. Fighting in the mountains and valleys, especially during the winter months in Korea, was taxing on all soldiers. So, the rotation of soldiers and units from the frontlines provided a needed reprieve.[307] A system of Rest and Relaxation (R&R) provided soldiers with a chance to get some hot rations, sleep, a nice shower or bath. Soldiers recharged their batteries. R&R was rejuvenating for the mind and body. Consequently, it was an amenity many soldiers looked forward to indulging in.[308]

Access to R&R depended upon whether or not a fighting unit and individual soldier was African-American or White. Williams asserts the 24th stayed out on the frontline longer than other infantry units. Williams recalled, "We were supposed to run all over Korea. We stayed on the line, at one time, seventy-two days straight."[309] As a result of remaining constantly on the frontline, instead of having spells of rest in the relative

---

[306] Ibid.

[307] Peter S. Kindsvatter, *American Soldiers: Ground Combat in the World Wars, Korea, and Vietnam* (Lawrence: University Press of Kansas, 2003), 93.

[308] Kindsvatter, *American Soldiers: Ground Combat in the World Wars, Korea, and Vietnam*, 94.

[309] James Williams. Interviewed by Eliot Pope. Personal Interview. Chicago, Illinois, January 12, 2015.

safety of the rear, the 24th became worn out. Tired and beaten down, the infantry was at a disadvantage when they encountered North Korean and Chinese soldiers.

Fatigued and unable to fight effectively, the unit was unaware not every unit fought as long or as hard as it did. Indeed, Williams learned the 24th was being mistreated only after he left the regiment. As he would later learn, "You were supposed to be on there for thirty days. I did not know that until I went to the White outfit."[310] Because the 24th stayed out on the frontline for twice as much time as a typical infantry unit, it became exhausted. The soldiers' experiences of staying on the frontlines for an extraordinary period of time reveals how institutional racism directly impacted them. With less rest than their White counterparts, the 24th was less prepared to fight against North Korean and Chinese soldiers.

Institutional racism shaped the regiment's time on the line, but so did the kinds of fronts they faced. Williams asserted the 24th was subjected to heavy combat more often than other infantries. As he put it, "Anywhere there is a hot spot at, that is where they are going to send the 24th. The 2nd division's being overrun. We got to go up there and pull them out there."[311] Williams's testimony reveals the 24th, at least from his perspective, was mismanaged by the U.S. military. With inferior weapons and with little time off to recharge, the unit was not given a chance to prove itself. Williams mentioned the decision to overwork the 24th without a

310 Ibid.
311 Ibid.

break, coupled with the decision to give them old weapons, set the unit up for failure. Williams's observations reveal the depth and breadth of institutional racism facing African-American soldiers during the war.

The institutional racism the 24th faced is corroborated by testimonies of White soldiers from the Korean War. According to Robert Barry, "We spent thirty days on the line under enemy fire."[312] After spending a month on the frontlines, he and his unit were pulled back to get some rest. As Barry put it, "it was thirty on and thirty off."[313] Barry's account reaffirms the point White units were given more time off than African-American units like the 24th. With more time off to rest, White units were able to recuperate from battle fatigue. Ultimately, this helped White units stay focused as they engaged with enemy combatants.

Additionally, the types of jobs African-American soldiers were assigned to in the U.S. military also reflected institutional racism. As Williams put it, the U.S. military "treated African-American soldiers bad."[314] He observed African-American soldiers "got all the shit detail and everything."[315] As he put it, "African-American guys would be riding around on the back of the garbage truck and White officers out there playing ball, eating ice cream."[316] In Williams's eyes, African-American soldiers had the least desirable and most labor intensive jobs. As Williams put it, if African-Americans "were mining coal out there. If it

[312]   Robert Barry. Interviewed by Nick Miller. Personal Interview. May 26, 2002.
[313]   Ibid.
[314]   James Williams. Interviewed by Eliot Pope. Personal Interview. Chicago, Illinois, January 12, 2015.
[315]   Ibid.
[316]   Ibid.

was one hundred guys out there shoveling coal, ninety-seven of them was colored."[317] The types of jobs available to African-American soldiers demonstrated they were not valued to the same degree as White soldiers. Most importantly, decisions to reserve the worst jobs for African-American soldiers reveals institutional racism.

In addition to the U.S. military's poor handling of the deployment of the 24th and the unfair distribution of heavy labor, some African-American soldiers faced abuse by their commanding officers. A. J. Nero's duty was to guard buildings during the war, a responsibility given to many soldiers. Nevertheless, unlike other soldiers, Nero was sometimes required to guard a building for several days at a time.[318] On one particular day, Nero was on duty all day.[319] As he recalls, "They put me on the post to guard, and around 6:00 p.m. nobody had come to relieve me."[320] He stayed at his post all night. When he went down to breakfast, his commanding officer said, "I need a runner today. All right, Nero, you are the runner." When Nero responded, "I was told I was getting my rest today, I was not relieved last night," his commanding officer replied, "You heard what I said. Get your rifle, let's go." [321] While Nero was following his orders, he was wounded. Nero's experience guarding a building for hours without a

---

317   Ibid.
318   A. J. Nero. Interviewed by Eliot Pope. Personal Interview. Chicago, Illinois, November 14, 2014. While Nero did see combat during the war, he acknowledged that most of his time was spent "in Korea, in a non-fighting situation."
319   Ibid.
320   Ibid.
321   Ibid.

break reflects the abusive and subtle nature of discrimination entrenched within the supposedly desegregated military.

One commonality of these stories of institutional racism is they go against normal military procedure. Indeed, both the example of deploying the 24th to the front for twice as long as White infantry units and Nero's directive to guard a building for an extended period of time were unusual. Significantly, such deviations from standard operating procedure reflect not only institutional racism, but also poor military management. For instance, Nero was wounded carrying out an order from his commanding officer to run an errand to the frontlines. With little sleep, he was more susceptible to making a mistake. Thus, the extraordinary demands the U.S. military placed on some African-American fighting units and individual soldiers indicate racism, both overt and covert, existed during the Korean War and effectively put the war effort at risk.

Subtle racism within the U.S. military often emerged through the decisions commanding White officers made which were racially motivated. According to Alan Gropman in *The Air Force Integrates: 1945 – 1964*, the Air Force's punishment of African-American air traffic controllers highlights racism within the U.S. Armed Forces. For example, Gropman notes, "Lieutenant General Partridge, Commander Far East Air Forces (FEAF), decided to remove African-Americans from duty as forward air controllers after several had twice misdirected fire on friendly troops."[322] General Partridge's decision was racially motivated. By punishing all African-American air traffic controllers because of the mistakes of a few, General Partridge rationalized all African-American air traffic controllers performed poorly. The decision to remove all air traffic controllers based on race rather than to focus on the individuals responsible for the accidents indicates racial discrimination permeated units beyond the 24th.

Physical violence against African-American soldiers as a result of racism was just as common as institutional racism and subtler forms of racism they experienced during the Korean War. For example, Clarence Senor highlights how some White soldiers used violence to intimidate African-Americans in his description of physical altercations while stationed in Korea. According to Senor, he was forced to defend himself from a racially motivated attack. After a White soldier from Alabama pushed him down to the ground, Senor got up and hit him.[323] Senor then said, "Where I come from, I do not care what you say. I get to hold my own."[324] Senor would not be bullied. He fought back. Reflecting on the incident, he believes the violence he experienced was an attempt to intimidate him. Although Senor refused to allow another soldier who harbored racist sentiments degrade him, his commanding officer expected such behavior. As a result of their altercation, Senor and the White soldier were

---

[322] Alan Gropman, *The Air Force Integrates: 1945-1964* (Washington, D.C.: Office of Air Force History, 1978), 147.

[323] Clarence Senor. Interviewed by Mark DePue. Springfield, Illinois, November 5, 2008.

[324] Ibid.

summoned to their captain. When they entered the captain's quarters, he turned and looked at Senor and said, "You people have to expect this from these guys."[325] In other words, the captain inferred African-American soldiers should assume they will be subjected to racially motivated violence while serving in the at least nominally desegregated military.

The captain's claim that race-based violence was inevitable also reflects a form of institutionalized racism. When the captain continued his lecture, however, Senor continued to resist. Senor insisted the White soldier "did not have no right to call him out of his name."[326] Seeking to defuse the situation, the captain said, "Yeah, but you have to expect that from them."[327] Incensed, Senor then violated protocol and insulted the captain, "Well, you son of a bitch, I do not need to."[328] Unaware of the irony, the captain said, "You cannot talk to me like that."[329] Senor responded by saying, "That's what I have been trying to tell you."[330] The captain turned red in the face and told Senor to "get on back to work."[331] Ultimately, neither Senor nor the White soldier were punished for the altercation. His story functions as a testament to the physical violence some African-American soldiers endured as a result of racism during the Korean War. Most importantly, it underscores how some African-Americans did seek to stand up for themselves against racial injustice.

---

[325] Ibid.
[326] Ibid.
[327] Ibid.
[328] Ibid.
[329] Ibid.
[330] Ibid.
[331] Ibid.

Senor's altercation with a fellow soldier is revealing because it high-lights two forms of racism: physical racism and institutionalized racism. First, the fight Senor had with the White soldier illustrates physical racism. The fact the White soldier assaulted Senor to "put him in his place" reveals the White soldier was a bigot. Second, the captain's response to the racially motivated fight underscores institutional racism. The captain's explana-tion the assault on him should be tolerated because the White soldier was from the South signifies the captain was giving tacit consent for the racially motivated attack. Moreover, since the captain was the judge and jury for this physical confrontation, his decision not to punish the White soldier for assaulting Senor was reflective of a willingness within the U.S. military to not address racism inflicted upon African-American soldiers. In effect, the captain's verdict to do nothing suggests discriminatory acts toward African-American soldiers were an accepted practice.

In spite of the racism African-American soldiers faced, they still served their country honorably during the Korean War. One example of the 24th's contribution is the significant sacrifices the unit made. During the Korean War, the regiment suffered heavy casualties. Curtis Morrow recalled the 24th endured higher causality rates juxtaposed to other fighting units within the U.S. military. According to him, the 24th "was composed of three thousand men, our regiment. One-third of them were killed in action. The exact figure was like nine hundred men were killed in action. That is not counting the wounded. Two-thirds were wounded seriously." [332] The 24th, like many other regiments, sustained heavy losses. Company B, another infantry unit within the regiment, sustained numerous casualties.[333] According to William Bowers, William Hammond, and George MacGarrigle, "Company B experienced twenty-six casualties among its officers and NCOs between July and September."[334] Just as other fighting units sustained high mortality rates, the 24th's high death rates suggests they fought just as hard and endured human loss just as much as White fighting units.

Along with the statistics, the nuances of the combat experiences of African-American soldiers are revealing. Their experiences demonstrate many African-American soldiers were perceptive warriors, able to pick up on subtleties within their environment. For instance, Curtis Morrow became keenly aware of the sights and smells around him during his service in Korea. As a scout in the U.S. Army, he developed a sixth sense. As Morrow put it, "We all got to smell them, you know. Everybody got different odors, body odors, and so it starts to hit the wind, and you could sense them, and you can smell them."[335]

---

332   Ibid.

333   William T. Bowers, William M. Hammond, and George L. MacGarrigle, *Black Soldier, White Army: The 24th Infantry Regiment in Korea* (Washington D.C.: Center of Military History, 1996), 75.

334   Bowers, Hammond and MacGarrigle, *Black Soldier, White Army: The 24th Infantry Regiment in Korea*, 267.

335   Curtis Morrow. Interviewed by Eliot Pope. Personal Interview. Chicago, Illinois, January 7, 2015. Jesse Jenkins. Interviewed by Eliot Pope. Personal Interview. Crown Point, Indiana, February 18, 2015. Jenkins stated that North Korean and Chinese soldiers ambushed U.S. Armed Forces often. According to Jenkins, "You would have roads full of refugees… people pushing baby carriages down the road. It might have been a baby in the carriage and they may not have been. It may have been a machine gun."

While Morrow's depiction of North Korean and Chinese soldiers as having a distinct smell was racist, his usage of this technique reveals the measures he took to protect himself and his unit from walking into ambushes set up by enemy combatants. By picking up on their scent, Morrow was able to fire at North Korean and Chinese soldiers who were hidden from the eye. His ability to identify the smell of North Korean and Chinese soldiers illustrates how some African-American soldiers used creative means to fight the enemy.

In addition to creativity, African-American soldiers also displayed an uncanny courage under fire as they engaged enemy combatants. In Lieutenant Colonel Bussey's autobiography entitled *Firefight at Yechon*, he illustrates the courage, sacrifice, and determination African-American soldiers displayed during the Battle of Yechon. As the first battle during the Korean War that United States, NATO and South Korean forces won, the importance of the conflict cannot be understated. Colonel Bussey remembered, "We continued to rain heavy fire from our hilltop. The enemy mortar stayed close on us, dumping shell fragments all around. I was ashamed of the slaughter before me, but this was my job, my duty, and my responsibility."[336] Colonel Bussey killed numerous North Koreans as he, along with his troops, took Yechon. As a result of their valor and courage under fire, the first Medal of Honor recipients were given out to members of the all-Black 24th. According to Colonel Bussey, "It is hard

---

[336] Charles M. Bussey, *Firefight at Yechon: Courage and Racism in the Korean War* (Riverside: Macmillan Publishing Co., 1991), 104.

for me to understand how the U.S. Army's official history could say the Battle of Yechon simply did not occur. I was there when the 25th Infantry Division Commander, Major General Kean, came to the regiment and pinned a Silver Star on my chest for my actions." [337] Colonel Bussey's military exploits indicates African-American soldiers risked their lives to defeat North Korean and Chinese soldiers.

Along with Colonel Bussey's autobiography, other men like James Lacy, a member of the 24th, highlight the bravery some African-American soldiers displayed during combat. Lacy's heroism saved his unit from being annihilated by North Korean and Chinese soldiers. The 24th was on the verge of being overrun by North Korean forces because one of its machine guns was malfunctioning. Captain Steinberg, Lacy's commanding officer, told him, "I need you to go up there and repair that machine gun because we are going to be attacked. Intelligence told us we are going to be attacked. I need that machine gun working, the second platoon." [338]

Lacy accepted the responsibility, telling Captain Steinberg, "I will go up there and repair it." [339] With two military escorts, Lacy made his way up to the machine gun. According to Lacy, "We maneuvered our way up to where the machine gun was. Got up there, and I am up there just feeling the way, and I repaired the machine gun." [340] Lacy returned to his camp after fixing the machine gun. As Lacy was returning to his

---

[337] Bussey, *Firefight at Yechon: Courage and Racism in the Korean War*, 108.

[338] James Lacy. Interviewed by Eliot Pope. Personal Interview. Chicago, Illinois, January 20, 2015.

[339] Ibid.

[340] Ibid.

camp, enemy troops started to attack the position without machine gun coverage. Lacy reported, "The North Koreans say, 'it is no machine gun coming from here, so that is the way we are going to hit.'"[341] The North Koreans, he later stated, "All got together, and they were going to come but I had fixed the machine gun, and it started shooting. It just started mowing them down."[342] Lacy was modest about his achievement but reported Captain Steinberg's appreciation. Lacy recalled, "The captain said, 'You saved a lot of guys because there is a machine gun for the first platoon, second platoon, third platoon. We do not have no machine gun in the fourth.'"[343] Captain Steinberg added, "I thank you for doing that, and I am going to give you a medal. I am going to put you in for a Silver Star because of all the guys you saved."[344] Lacy was elated. However, due to unforeseen circumstances, Lacy was not acknowledged by the U.S. military for his military accomplishments.

During the battle, North Korean scouts studied the 24th. They analyzed the troop movements of the infantry. They studied their uniforms and observed their interactions with one another. They surveyed the perimeter of the 24th's camp and identified weak points. They memorized how many guards were on patrol during the day and at night. They knew when their shifts ended and began. North Korean scouts even discovered where soldiers of the 24th slept in their camp. After North Korean battle-

[341] Ibid.
[342] Ibid.
[343] Ibid.
[344] Ibid.

field commanders scrutinized this information, they concluded Captain Steinberg was an invaluable leader of the 24th who had to be killed. North Korean officers determined murdering Captain Steinberg would weaken the 24th's resolve to carry on fighting. So, North Korean strategists began plotting his assassination. Based on intelligence and data compiled by scouts, they decided on when, where and how Captain Steinberg would be slain. Afterward, North Korean military officers selected a soldier who had the requisite skill set to accomplish this risky mission. They needed someone who had a good memory, capable of killing in a discreet, efficient manner, could blend in with U.S., NATO and South Korean army personnel and who could enter and exit the 24th's basecamp without being noticed.

In the dead of night, a North Korean soldier slipped undetected past armed guards who were positioned at the outskirts of the 24th's base camp. After taking a few moments to recall where the captain was located, the soldier crept over to Captain Steinberg and noticed he was asleep. The enemy combatant quietly took out his bayonet, raised it above his head and with all his might drove it into Captain Steinberg's rib cage. The Captain gasped for air and then started coughing up blood. Moments later he died. The assassin then discreetly left the camp, leaving no trace behind.

The next morning Captain Steinberg's men found him on the ground in a pool of fresh blood with a bayonet plunged deep in his chest. Lacy reminisced, "He was a good captain though, Captain Steinberg, very good man, but never got a chance to put me up for that medal. I just forgot about it, I just said, 'Well, that is all right.'"[345] Because of the death of his captain, Lacy's heroics during battle were not acknowledged by the U.S. military. Nonetheless, Lacy's training with machine guns and the risk he took to save the lives of the men in his unit are reflective of his bravery, the quality of training he received and his competence as a soldier.

Other African-American soldiers were equally willing to fight hard and sacrifice their lives to defend their country. For example, Walter Dowdy recalls getting wounded by mortar fire during the Korean War.[346] He was coming down a hill when, as he says, "*Bam*. Everything was black. I felt something running down my face." Dowdy immediately passed out. He was then taken to a hospital and treated for his injuries. Dowdy's injury reveals the sacrifice some African-American soldiers made as they engaged with enemy combatants.

Similarly, Roy Dell Johnson was driving in a convoy from Pusan when it was suddenly ambushed. During the encounter with North Korean soldiers, a bullet went through Johnson's "cheek, and it came out [his] lip."[347] Johnson was sent to a hospital, treated for his injuries, and

---

[345]   Ibid.

[346]   Walter Lee Dowdy. Interviewed by Michael Willie. Personal Interview. Chattanooga, Tennessee, February 18, 2004.

[347]   Roy Dell Johnson. Interviewed by Eliot Pope. Personal Interview. Arlington, Texas, March 2, 2015. Oral history testimonies reveal how some African-American soldiers paid with their lives fighting for America. John Thomas' experiences in Korea include the loss of his friend. According to Thomas, "I was in a foxhole one time with my buddy, in a foxhole, and we were fighting at the enemy, and all of a sudden I noticed he had slumped over, and I thought he was sleep. I thought he was asleep or whatever, so I looked down and he was gone." John Thomas. Interview by Brianna Brooks. Personal Interview. Indianapolis, Indiana, October 4, 2009. In effect, some oral history testimonies reveal the bravery and sacrifice displayed by African-American soldiers during combat in the Korean War.

sent back to the frontlines. Due to Johnson's fighting prowess, he would be wounded several more times in combat operations. In fact, Johnson was wounded on three separate occasions. African-American soldiers were on the frontline and were risking injury and death with regularity. The wartime injuries described by African-American soldiers such as Dowdy and Johnson indicate they were willing to sacrifice their lives for their country.

Details of bloody engagements between African-American troops and North Korean and Chinese soldiers provide further evidence African-American soldiers served honorably. For instance, Johnson describes meeting fierce resistance when he landed at Inchon along with other American soldiers. According to Johnson, North Koreans subjected American troops to heavy artillery fire upon their landing. With bullets flying and mortars exploding, Americans suffered heavy losses as they sought to secure the beach and surrounding area at Inchon.

Johnson remembered the landing as "A horrible sight, you know. The—the thing looking like Kool-Aid out there. On your . . . [It was] red, man." [348] Johnson recalls the Battle of Inchon "was very, very stressful." [349] During this violent campaign, Johnson "got a big, big piece of shrapnel" lodged in his body. [350] Despite his wounds, Johnson took part in the

---

This portrayal of African-American soldiers in combat refutes a strand of historiography that asserts African-American soldiers were of poor quality.

[348]   Ibid.

[349]   Ibid.

[350]   Ibid.

United Nations military push which threw the North Koreans back to the Chosin Reservoir.

A.J. Nero, a platoon leader who earned his Purple Heart after he was wounded in battle, tells a similar story of honorable service in combat. During Nero's first day in combat, he was wounded. Nero reported, "My squad leader asked me [if I knew] that my weapon was not firing. I told him, 'Yes, I know it.'"[351] Later, after Nero had fixed his weapon, his commanding officer was still not convinced he had a working weapon and asked for proof. He said, "Show me."[352] Accordingly, Nero pointed his gun at a stone in the middle of the frontline.[353] Nevertheless, Nero's squad leader redirected him and told him to "shoot it over in the enemy line" because "you might hit one of the Gooks."[354]

Nero fired his gun pursuant to his squad leader's direction. In response, however, a North Korean soldier fired back, "chipping the dirt right in front of" Nero.[355] Vulnerable and exposed, Nero, along with the rest of his squad, pulled back from their position and started to run away. Then, North Korean soldiers started to chase them while at the same time firing their weapons at Nero's squad. Nero recalled, "We took off, but they caught us. They killed him, but I got wounded and about six others [did,

---

[351] A. J. Nero. Interviewed by Eliot Pope. Personal Interview. Chicago, Illinois, November 14, 2014.
[352] Ibid.
[353] Ibid.
[354] Ibid.
[355] Ibid.

too]. Just a little thing like that happened. "[356] African-American soldiers were in the heart of combat and fought valiantly.

Just as African-Americans had to endure various types of racism during the Korean War, African-American soldiers had to address moral dilemmas which tested their faith and had an impact on their psyche. James Lacy's defense mechanism shaped his recollection of his participation in violent encounters with North Korean and Chinese soldiers. Lacy's description of the role he played in violent engagements with enemy combatants minimizes his involvement in the encounters he participated in. When asked if he had ever killed anybody during his tenure as a soldier, he said, "Yes." Nonetheless, as a machine gunner, he stated Captain Steinberg, not he, set the setting on his machine gun. As Lacy put it, "During the day they would fix it, so it [would] only go this far and this way. I could only go where they got it fixed. The captain had somebody to fix it."[357]

When the North Koreans and Chinese attacked, Captain Steinberg said, "OK, Lacy, give them a burst."[358] Upon that command, Lacy would climb on his jeep, got behind his Browning M1919 .30 caliber machine gun, and had "the guys get down in the hole because he was going to shoot over their heads. He then started shooting."[359] A kettle drum sound, coupled with the smell of gun smoke, filled the air as Lacy mowed down

---

[356]   Ibid. A.J. Nero's shrapnel injury was a common injury among many U.S. soldiers. James Wiggins, for example, was hit by shrapnel on July the 13, 1950. He later had to leave the Korean War after he injured his left leg and left foot.

[357]   James Lacy. Interviewed by Eliot Pope. Personal Interview. Chicago, Illinois, January 20, 2015.

[358]   Ibid.

[359]   Ibid.

Chinese and North Korean soldiers. Lacy became proficient at killing enemy combatants, saving the lives of countless U.S. soldiers. However, he consistently found ways to avoid moral responsibility for taking the lives of the enemy.

One device Lacy employed for avoiding responsibility for killing was minimizing his role in killing enemy combatants. When Lacy was congratulated by fellow soldiers for his skill as a machine gunner, he would reply, "Yeah, well, Captain set the machine gun. He knew where they were. He had to set the machine gun and all I did was shoot over you all's head."[360] By emphasizing Captain Steinberg had set his machine gun, Lacy displaced some of the blame for the killing of enemy combatants from himself onto his commanding officer. When Lacy was asked, "Well, how many you kill last night?"[361] he would reply, "No, no, I do not want to know."[362]

Lacy admitted, "I do not want to know because I know that if I did not get this people coming this way, they would get these guys sitting in the hole there. I never did want to know."[363] Lacy's response is revealing. His decision not to find out how many men he had killed helped him separate himself from carrying out his duties as a machine gunner. Assigning responsibility to Captain Steinberg and refusing to find out how many people he killed on the battlefield helped him continue to do his job.

---

[360]   Ibid.
[361]   Ibid.
[362]   Ibid.
[363]   Ibid.

The job of a soldier is to kill enemy combatants through the use of force.[364] Yet, some violent encounters during the Korean War were more complicated than shooting North Korean and Chinese combatants on the battlefield. James Williams's encounter with people he thought were enemy combatants serves as an example of the complexities of armed combat. While clearing out a small town with fellow soldiers, Williams and his fellow soldiers came upon a series of huts they believed were filled with enemy soldiers. Hicks, a member of Williams's group, used a flame-thrower to set the huts on fire and flush out the occupants. According to Williams, "When he fired down there and hit that, it set all of them on fire. That is when they started coming up out of there. Then I saw four coming up out of there."[365] The four individuals Williams saw were Korean women who he thought were armed. Williams took action. Standing behind his machine gun, he opened fire. Riddled with bullets, the women immediately fell to the ground. Bright, red blood stained the earth and soaked their clothes. The aroma of smoke and the metallic rusty smell of blood filled the air. They died moments later. As Williams explained, "These folks [were coming] up out of there but they had weapons in their hands, like this, coming up out, so I cut them down."[366] Because Williams could not distinguish whether or not the four women were enemy combatants,

---

[364] Richard Holmes, *Acts of War: The Behavior of Men in Battle* (New York: Simon and Schuster, 1985), 31. According to Holmes, "the soldier's primary function, the use—or threatened use—of force, sets him apart from civilians" (31).

[365] James Williams. Interviewed by Eliot Pope. Personal Interview. Chicago, Illinois, January 12, 2015.

[366] Ibid. James Williams's commanding officer observed the bodies of the dead Koreans and determined that Williams was at fault. His commanding officer stated that he was under arrest, but Williams remained at the scene heavily armed. Williams was ultimately acquitted of any wrongdoing.

he made a split-second decision to kill them. Consequently, Williams was court-martialed but later acquitted for shooting and killing the women.

Williams's defensive response to killing four North Korean women indicates he developed a callousness regarding certain traumatic events he participated in during the fog of war. Before Williams told his story of killing four North Korean women, he stated a colonel told him to "Kill every son of a bitch who jumps up in front of you because if you do not kill him, he is damn sure going to kill you."[367] Williams took those instructions to heart. This advice became a guiding principle he referred to time and time again as he engaged with enemy combatants. Internalizing this order gave Williams the strength to take decisive action during battle, even if those split-second decisions took innocent lives. This draconian approach to war helped Williams stay alive while also potentially robbing him of his humanity. A "kill or be killed" mentality explains why Williams opened fire on the women who appeared to be carrying weapons and demonstrates how he was able to come to peace with that decision.

Although Williams was decisive in the heat of the moment, his response to the news he would be court-martialed reveals he believed his actions were justified. When Williams's commanding officer confronted him, he stated, "I am not paying too much attention to what he is saying because I had just come out of a big firefight. We got everything cleared away down there and moved on up." [368] Once he considered the possibil-

---

[367]   Ibid.
[368]   Ibid.

ity of a court-martial, however, Williams became angry with his captain. Describing his reaction sixty years after the incident, he said, "Next firefight we get into, I am going to kill that son of a bitch."[369] Williams was infuriated at the possibility of punishment for an action he believed was warranted. In his mind, he made the right call by eliminating targets which he deemed a potential threat. Even if Williams made a tragic mistake in the heat of the moment, his embrace of the "kill or be killed" ideology desensitized him to the fact that he executed four unarmed women in cold blood. His lack of emotion underscores how this ideology suppressed any remorse or regret Williams might have possessed after this unconscionable event took place.

External psychological warfare as waged by the enemy was, for many soldiers, met by internal moral quandaries. While Williams's killing of four women who he believed were carrying guns highlights his ruthlessness during battle, other experiences Williams had during the Korean War offer a glimpse of his humanity. For example, he describes being stationed next to a river by a hill while on duty when he saw North Korean refugees coming over a hill.[370] According to Williams, "It was like, maybe, one thousand of them. If there was one thousand of them, three hundred to four hundred of them would be Chinese in there."[371] The U.S. Army could not allow the refugees to cross the river because of the possibility of enemy combatants hidden within the group. Therefore, Williams, along

---

[369]   Ibid.
[370]   James Williams. Interviewed by Eliot Pope. Personal interview. Chicago, Illinois, January 12, 2015.
[371]   Ibid.

with other army personnel, "went down there, talked to them people, told them to go back, they could not come over. They said, 'OK.'"[372] A few minutes later the Korean refugees again started to approach the U.S. position. Williams and other army personnel again "went down there and talked to them. Went back up there. When we got back up there this time, the captain told the platoon leaders to pass the word down then [if] they start moving again, fire for effect."[373] The captain's directive was simple—kill the Korean refugees if they came toward the line again. To Williams's relief, the refugees went back over the hill, defusing a potentially deadly situation.

While this encounter with North Korean refugees did not end in violence, the event did affect Williams emotionally. As he put it, "That was what got me. I had to kill all these people. I will remember that until the day I die."[374] As Williams made this statement, he started to choke up. He had faced a tough decision. If he was given an order to kill the North Korean refugees but refused, he would have risked getting court-martialed. If he had followed through with the order, he would most likely have killed innocent civilians and would have had to live with those emotions for the rest of his life. Later, Williams stated, "If you get the order to fire, you fire. I was going to fire. I was hoping the good Lord would kill me."[375] After Williams said this, he started to cry uncontrollably. These

---

[372]   Ibid.
[373]   Ibid. During the interview, James Williams's voice trembled.
[374]   Ibid. This statement suggests Williams did not want to face this issue.
[375]   Ibid.

breakdowns reveal his humanity. For Williams, killing innocent civilians was a nearly unspeakable act. Yet, if given the order, he would have killed, even though it went against his values.

Some soldiers faced moral dilemmas as it related to their treatment of prisoners of war. James Lacy's treatment of a prisoner of war (POW) showcases his desire to carry out his duty as a soldier while also maintaining a sense of humanity. He related an incident which took place on a battlefield in Korea. While in his jeep on a hill, he came across a North Korean soldier who wanted to surrender. Lacy jumped off his jeep and searched the soldier. According to Lacy, who accompanied his narrative with physical gestures, "After I assessed him, I got him out and tied his hands together like this, so he could not run away."[376] Once he had the POW in restraints, Lacy began looking after the man's needs. Lacy recalled, "I went to get my sack and found something with rice in it. I took it, opened it up, and I did not want to untie his hand, so I fed him. I fed him."[377] Lacy also got his prisoner some water. The next morning Lacy went to Post Command and asked them, "What do you want me to do with the prisoner?"[378] Post Command told Lacy, "You captured him, go down that road and take him to the prison camp."[379] Lacy proceeded to take his prisoner to the prison camp in a manner respectful of the man's humanity.

---

[376] James Lacy. Interviewed by Eliot Pope. Personal Interview. Chicago, Illinois, January 20, 2015.
[377] Ibid.
[378] Ibid.
[379] Ibid.

While Lacy's treatment of the POW underscored his compassion toward the man, some soldiers did not view his supervision of the North Korean favorably. As Lacy walked the POW to the prison camp, he ran into some fellow soldiers. As Lacy relates, one of them said, "'Hey, put that gun on the guy.' I said, 'He is no problem.'" Despite Lacy's response, the soldiers took Lacy's POW, put him on his knees and hit him in the back with the butt of his rifle.[380] Lacy said, "'Hey, there is no use in all that, he is not a problem'" and explained he "had him half of the night."[381] Lacy again stated, "He gave me no problems."[382] Lacy's testimony notwithstanding, the soldiers responded, "Hey but that is just not the way you treat a prisoner. You supposed to be rough with him."[383] Lacy said, "Not me, not me."[384] Lacy refused to take part in the abuse and humiliation of this POW, but the experience affected him deeply.

The difference between Lacy's treatment of the POW and that of his comrades uncovers his humanity. His description of how he treated the POW reveals his kindness, and the food and water he got for the prisoner illustrates his generosity. Lacy's unwillingness to put a gun on the prisoner of war as he was escorting him highlights the bond forged between them. Finally, Lacy's refusal to beat the POW, even though other soldiers claimed it was appropriate to do so, reveals his sense of fairness. Thus, his story frames him as a responsible warrior. Even though he had the power to hurt

---

[380] Ibid.
[381] Ibid.
[382] Ibid.
[383] Ibid.
[384] Ibid.

his prisoner, he declined to do so. In this way, Lacy was able to maintain a sense of decency through his humane treatment of the prisoner of war.

In the chaos of war, maintaining a sense of humanity and, above all, sanity was a struggle for many soldiers. Organized religion, however, helped soldiers cope with and process the horrors of war. Lacy revealed he prayed often for protection from enemy attacks.[385] Many soldiers relied on faith to help them cope with the stresses of war.[386] Soldiers "expected, or at least prayed for, exactly that — they wanted God to spare them."[387] More to the point, soldiers were less focused on achieving salvation and more interested in God shielding them from serious injury or death from shrapnel, bullets, mortar shells or bombs.[388] Some soldiers believed their faith in God provided them with a cloak of invincibility which helped them carry out their duties.

The decision to embrace religion often came when soldiers first encountered enemy combatants in armed struggles. As Curtis Morrow put it, "All atheists become believers after their first serious engagement with the enemy, after the first time they experience a barrage of enemy artillery or mortar fire."[389] Embracing religion became a necessity for some soldiers. It gave them hope. It gave them inspiration to carry on and endure. In fact, some soldiers' piety was infectious. As bombs rained

---

[385]   Ibid.

[386]   Peter S. Kindsvatter, *American Soldiers: Ground Combat in the World Wars, Korea, and Vietnam* (Lawrence: University Press of Kansas, 2003), 115.

[387]   Kindsvatter, *American Soldiers: Ground Combat in the World Wars, Korea, and Vietnam*, 115.

[388]   Ibid.

[389]   Curtis Morrow, *What's a Commie Ever Done to Black People? A Korean War Memoir of Fighting in the U.S. Army's Last All Negro Unit* (Jefferson: McFarland and Company, 1979), 114.

down from the sky, Lacy and others dropped down on one knee and started digging a foxhole.[390] As the bombs got closer to their position, men started to dig for their lives. Men started crying. Others began to vomit. Some even urinated in their pants. As a devout Catholic, Lacy was asked, "Are you saying those Catholic prayers?" by other soldiers. Lacy said, "Yes." The soldier then told Lacy, "You are not saying them loud enough!" Lacy then said, "Hail Mary, Full of grace, The Lord is with thee. Blessed art thou among women, and blessed is the fruit of thy womb, Jesus. Holy Mary, Mother of God, pray for us sinners now, and at the hour of our death. Amen."[391] As he said his prayer over and over again, other men began to follow along, saying the prayer in unison with Lacy. The men's anxiety gradually dissipated. Miraculously, the bombs became less loud. Most importantly, the projectiles did not hurt Lacy or any of his fellow soldiers.[392]

Despite the seemingly insurmountable odds they faced, African-American soldiers endured and, in some instances, prevailed. They found unique ways to stay warm and dry. Some soldiers devised ways to sleep while marching. Others used their armpits to dry out their socks so as to avoid getting trench foot. They used smell, for example, to track enemy combatants. African-American soldiers maintained their dignity and self-respect in the face of racist soldiers and officers who sought to belittle them. They figured out how to fix broken machine guns just before

---

[390] James Lacy. Interviewed by Eliot Pope. Personal Interview. Chicago, Illinois, January 20, 2015.
[391] Ibid.
[392] Ibid.

enemy combatants overran their position and killed when they deemed it necessary. While these stories of African-American soldiers during combat are distinctly different, the common theme which links them together is survival. African-American soldiers learned how to navigate through a spider web of different challenges in order to stay alive.

Given the unique ways in which African-American soldiers addressed the numerous mental, physical and emotional tests they faced, they exceeded expectations. Ensign Jesse Brown could have opted not to become a naval pilot, but despite prevailing winds of racism became a naval aviator. African-American soldiers could have surrendered to the cold, but many did not. They could have given up against battle-hardened North Korean and Chinese soldiers, but most stood and fought, even with inferior weapons. They could have succumbed to resentment and anger, especially as they endured unfair treatment as a result of various forms of racism, but they continued to carry on and serve their country honorably. African-American soldiers overcame these obstacles, and in doing so became unsung heroes of the Korean War.

CHAPTER 4
Crusade

While Ensign Jesse Brown's heroic death paints a picture of interracial solidarity during the Korean War, racial anxiety boiling beneath the surface ensured African-American and White soldiers would not whole heartedly come together. Racism within the U.S. military legal system during the Korean War was yet another battle African-American soldiers had to fight in order to protect their dignity and self-worth as servicemen within the U.S. military. The perception African-American soldiers did not measure up to the expectations of the U.S. military was underscored by the high number of African-American soldiers who were court-martialed, often on dubious charges, juxtaposed to their White counterparts. To address these attempted character assassinations waged by some White servicemen against African-American soldiers, Thurgood Marshall, working on behalf of the National Association for the Advancement of Colored People (NAACP), protected many African-American soldiers' reputations by undermining the legitimacy of the court-martials they faced.

Before Marshall's landmark investigation, African-American soldiers were, in fact, praised for their fighting capabilities. The 24th's valiant efforts at the Battle of Yechon, which took place on July 28th, 1950, suggested African-American soldiers were competent soldiers who could be depended on in a firefight. They fought bravely. The victory at Yechon also had strategic value for the United States as it was "the first sizable ground victory in the Korean War."[393] Consequently, Yechon helped to initially establish African-American soldiers' reputation as good, quality soldiers.

Despite this reputation African-American soldiers earned at the outset of the Korean War, the idea that they were ill-prepared has dominated the overall narrative of the all-Black 24th. Something seemed off. Before Marshall left Korea, he had an opportunity to spend some time with the soldiers of the 24th. He wanted to know the truth. Marshall believed these men had insider information on why there was a disproportionate number of court-martials of African-American soldiers from the 24th. Some African-American soldiers reported to Marshall that White commanding officers told them repeatedly, "I despise nigger troops. I do not want to command you or any other niggers. This division is no good, and you are lousy. You do not know how to fight."[394] These words cut to the bone of why African-Americans in the 24th performed poorly – they were

---

[393] Gerald Astor, *The Right to Fight: A History of African-Americans in the Military* (Boston: De Capo Press, 2001), 353.

[394] Astor, *The Right to Fight: A History of African-Americans in the Military*, 140.

not respected or valued. Held in contempt by White commanding officers, the low expectations of African-American soldiers sent a clear message — they meant nothing and their service to their country meant even less. Sadly, African-American soldiers of the 24th were expected to fail.

The inordinate number of court-martials of African-American soldiers reflected the lack of respect the U.S. military had for them. In total, thirty-nine African-American soldiers were tried and convicted in court-martials which were held in Korea.[395] Most court-martial convictions of African-American soldiers indicated they were in violation of the ninety–ninth Article of War, "misbehavior in the presence of the enemy."[396] In response to their convictions, these men requested the NAACP investigate their cases.

Founded in 1909, the NAACP was a powerful advocate for civil rights within the African-American community, often leading grass-roots movements which advocated for securing equal opportunities for African-Americans within employment, education, and housing.[397] The focus of the NAACP is to make sure the rights highlighted in the Thirteenth Amendment, which ended slavery, Fourteenth Amendment, which contends that people born or naturalized in the United States are citizens, and Fifteenth Amendment, which ensures a person can vote regardless of race, creed or color, were being upheld by the U.S. Constitution. Given

---

[395]   Thurgood Marshall, "Summary Justice – The Negro GI in Korea," *The Crisis*, May 1951, 297.

[396]   "NAACP Gives GIs Priority," *The Chicago Defender*, December 1950, 12.

[397]   "2020 Nation's Premier Civil Rights Organization," National Association for the Advancement of Colored People, accessed on July 2, 2021, https://naacp.org/nations-premier-civil-rights-organization/.

the NAACP's mission, the organization was well positioned to address the needs of the thirty-nine African-American soldiers who were court-martialed. Ultimately, Marshall was chosen to represent the NAACP in Korea in hopes of overturning these convictions.

The NAACP could not have picked a better man to take on the U.S. military and the court-martials it doled out to African-American soldiers at an alarming rate. Marshall was smart, observant, witty and detailed. Like Asa Randolph, Marshall's strength of character was forged in his home. He grew up in a family that valued standing up for yourself, even in the face of powerful Whites. Marshall's parents, Norma and Willie Marshall, provided a middle-class environment for their children. Like many African-American families, extended families, not the nuclear family, often raised their children. The dictum "it takes a village to raise a child" applied to Marshall's family. When they moved in with Marshall's Uncle Fearless Williams in Baltimore, Marshall found an individual who would have a significant impact on the trajectory of his life.[398]

Uncle Williams had a good job as a personal assistant to the President of the Baltimore and Ohio Railroad (B&O), the oldest railroad in the United States. [399] He organized the B&O President's itinerary and served him lunch.[400] Uncle Williams was a "tall, broad-shouldered, wide smiling man…. A sort of major domo in the office of the president."[401] He was well

---

[398] Juan Williams, *Thurgood Marshall: America's Revolutionary* (New Times: Broadway Books, 1995), 28.
[399] Williams, *Thurgood Marshall: America's Revolutionary*, 28.
[400] Ibid.
[401] Ibid.

connected, with strong relationships with powerful White businessmen and political leaders.[402] Uncle Williams' mixture of industriousness and joviality increased his likability. "Fearless was the most important African-American in the B&O Railroad," according to Douglas C. Turnbull, Jr., Executive Assistant to the President of B&O Railroad for a number of years.[403] Uncle Williams set a great example for Marshall and left a memorable impression on his young nephew.[404]

Just as Uncle Williams helped to shape Marshall's personality, his parents, Norma and Willie, also had an impact on Marshall. Norma came from a family of educators. Her mother and sister were both kindergarten teachers, so she looked to follow in their footsteps. Norma enrolled in classes at Morgan College in 1921.[405] Clearly driven, Norma wanted to succeed. She superimposed those expectations onto her sons, Thurgood and Aubrey. Norma wanted to make sure her sons had as many opportunities as she had, so she put pressure on them to perform academically.[406]

Like Norma, Willie also wanted to make sure his children received the best education. However, the two diverged in terms of how they sought to motivate their children academically. While Norma looked to set an example for her sons to follow by getting her certification to teach, Willie often used threats to encourage his children to excel in school. Willie's motivation techniques originated from "his lack of schooling"

---

[402] Ibid.
[403] Ibid.
[404] Ibid.
[405] Ibid.
[406] Ibid.

which he believed limited his options in life to being a Pullman Porter.[407] Consequently, Willie overcompensated for not having a good education by demanding his children be well educated.

Of Willie's many passions, his interest in the law left a lasting impression on Marshall. In his spare time, Willie frequently went to courtrooms to observe trials. He watched lawyers represent their clients by presenting eloquent arguments which portrayed them in a positive light. He observed them build their cases with evidence. He saw attorneys ask witnesses incisive questions designed to help them win their cases. When he got home, "He would use lawyers' tactics on both sons during arguments at the dinner table, demanding that they logically back up any claim they made, while discussing politics or even the weather."[408] Through these heated exchanges, Marshall's father forced him to process arguments and react to them in real time.[409] Unbeknownst to Marshall, Willie was helping to lay the foundation for his son's critical thinking skills. Marshall would later on in life depend on these cognitive skills to win cases in the Supreme Court. These legal victories would improve the quality of life for African-Americans and cement Marshall's legacy as a champion for civil rights.

Marshall's communication skills would continue to improve while he was in high school. When he joined the debate team, his verbal skills were further enhanced. In fact, he emerged as the most effective debater

---

[407]   Ibid., 34.
[408]   Ibid., 35.
[409]   Ibid.

on the team.[410] Marshall's feisty, argumentative style garnered respect from his debate coach, Gough McDaniels. McDaniels encouraged Marshall to always be prepared before a debate. He made Marshall do in-depth research on topics for upcoming debates.[411] The lessons Marshall learned from McDaniels would later be used to help him construct arguments which would undermine the creditability of court-martials faced by African-American soldiers during the Korean War.

After college, Marshall set his sights on going to law school. University of Maryland's Law School was right down the street from his house in Baltimore, making it an ideal choice. Marshall was seriously considering applying to the University of Maryland's Law School, even though the school had only graduated two African-American students in its history. Beyond that, no African-Americans had been admitted to the school since the 1890s.[412] Even so, Marshall applied to the University of Maryland Law School but was rejected. If it were not for his race, the University of Maryland's Law School would have been an ideal choice. Marshall was a gifted student who undoubtedly would have thrived at the University of Maryland's Law School. He was angry but undeterred. Despite his rejection, Marshall did not give up hope. With no other options available to him, he opted to go to Howard University School of Law, which was at once inexpensive and taught the law to African-American students in a

---

[410] Ibid., 36.
[411] Ibid.
[412] Ibid., 52.

supportive, nurturing environment.[413] Due to segregation policies, aspiring African-American lawyers by default were forced to attend Howard. In doing so, the school had the distinct honor of developing some of the best legal minds in the African-American community.

Among the many talented and gifted African-American lawyers who came out of Howard, Marshall was one of the best. When he entered law school, he met Dean Charles Houston — a stern, no-nonsense administrator. Dean Houston warned the entering freshman "Their success in college meant nothing to him, and it would give him great pleasure to flunk out Phi Beta Kappas." [414] He later told them, "Each one of you look at the man to your right and then look to the man on your left. Realize that two of you will not be here next year."[415] The message was clear. Expectations were high. No corners would be cut. Marshall got the point.

When Marshall entered Howard, America was suffering from the Great Depression. Job opportunities, especially for African-Americans, were few. As a result, Marshall was dependent on his family for survival. Vivian, Marshall's wife, worked to support him. His mother, Norma, even sold "valuables to help with his tuition."[416] Given these circumstances, Marshall had no choice but to work hard to get the best possible grades in law school. So, on train rides to and from Baltimore, he immersed himself in law books. Marshall recalled, "All of my notes I would take down in the

---

[413] Ibid., 53.
[414] Ibid.
[415] Ibid.
[416] Ibid.

book by hand and that night I would type them up after I rode back to Baltimore."[417] Marshall's work ethic, at this point in his life, was legendary.

Howard proved to be a stimulating intellectual environment. Law students at Howard were exposed to some of the best, brightest, and most ambitious legal minds in the United States. These legal scholars and professors introduced new ideas, political theories, and unique ways of interpreting the law. Academics like Roscoe Pound, Dean of Harvard Law School; Clarence Darrow, revered for his work with the Scopes Monkey trial; Arthur Hayes of the American Civil Liberties Union (ACLU); and John Davis of South Carolina, who ran for President of the United States in 1924, together helped to broaden and deepen the intellectual curiosity of students enrolled at Howard University.[418]

After Marshall graduated from law school, he took the Maryland bar exam and passed it on the first try. He then opened his own law firm. Given that he opened his law firm during the Great Depression, money was tight. Unemployment in Baltimore "was over twenty percent, even higher among African-Americans."[419] Survival was key. Marshall, for instance, was forced to bring leftovers for lunch to work. Despite his frugality, he still lost three thousand five hundred dollars in his first year.[420] Things were rough for Marshall, but they would get better.

---

[417]   Ibid.

[418]   Ibid., 57.

[419]   Jo Ann E. Argersinger, *Toward a New Deal in Baltimore* (Chapel Hill: University of North Carolina Press, 1988), 30.

[420]   Juan Williams, *Thurgood Marshall: America's Revolutionary* (New Times: Broadway Books, 1995), 28.

In the 1940s, Marshall's fortunes would improve. He would win a number of key cases, which bolstered his reputation. In 1940, he successfully defended four convicted African-American men who had confessed they committed a murder, even though they did not do it.[421] In *Shelley vs. Kraemer*, the Supreme Court "struck down the legality of racially restrictive housing covenants."[422] And, in *Sweatt vs. Painter*, a case which challenged "separate but equal," the Supreme Court sided with Heman Sweatt, a man who was denied entry into University of Texas School of Law because he was African-American.[423] Marshall's legal victories, particularly in the realm of combating racism, foreshadowed the work he would do on behalf of the NAACP on court-martial cases of African-American soldiers.

The NAACP was first notified of the excessive number of African-American soldiers facing court-martials through pleas from thirty-nine GIs and their family members. They were soliciting the NAACP to investigate institutional racism they believed was embedded within their trials.[424] In their eyes, the NAACP was their best hope to get the court-martials dismissed.[425] Luckily, the NAACP accepted their request. The NAACP declared it would "Defend, upon determination of racial discrimination or denial of constitutional rights, any of the convicted

---

[421]   "Thurgood Marshall," History, accessed on July 10, 2020, https://www.history.com/topics/black-history/thurgood-marshall.

[422]   Ibid.

[423]   Ibid.

[424]   Marshall, Thurgood. Interviewed by Ed Erwin. April 13th, 1977. transcript, Columbia Center for Oral History, Columbia University. New York, NY.

[425]   "GIs Convicted in Korea Ask NAACP Aid," *The Chicago Defender*, November 1950, 25.

servicemen who request such assistance."[426] Once the NAACP agreed to investigate the court-martials of African-Americans soldiers who served in Korea, the organization immediately reached out to Marshall.

Before Marshall took his trip to Japan to take on the court-martials, the U.S. State Department sought to stop him. The State Department wanted to block the trip because they wanted "to manage the activities of African-Americans overseas."[427] In other words, the State Department wanted to stop activist, legal experts and others from potentially undermining the U.S. military and its war effort in Korea. On a broader level, the State Department aimed to control the narrative of America within the international community by limiting travel for prominent African-American academics and scholars who might challenge the nation's image. Paul Robeson and W.E.B. Dubois both, for example, "had their passports confiscated and had been denied access to an international audience for their civil rights appeals."[428] In other words, the U.S. State Department was seeking to manage the perception of how racial inequality within the United States was viewed by the international community.

In addition to the State Department looking for ways to block Marshall from going to Tokyo, General Douglas MacArthur also sought to stop him from taking the trip. General MacArthur was a towering figure within the U.S. military. He was a complex blend of ego, ambition,

---

[426]   "NAACP Gives GIs Priority," *The Chicago Defender*, December 1950, 12.

[427]   Lu Sun, "Battling the Military Jim Crow: Thurgood Marshall and the Racial Politics of the NAACP During the Korean War" MA thesis, Vanderbilt University, 2014), 16.

[428]   Sun, *Battling the Military Jim Crow: Thurgood Marshall and the Racial Politics of the NAACP During the Korean War*, 16.

brilliance and recklessness.[429] General MacArthur was the grandson of a Milwaukee judge, who also happened to be a personal friend of President Lincoln. Beyond that, he was the son of a revered Medal of Honor recipient who led "his Wisconsin regiment up the face of Missionary Ridge during the Civil War."[430] Given his family's pedigree, General MacArthur was destined for greatness.

Along with his family lineage, General MacArthur's credentials, both in academia and on the battlefield, were noteworthy. He thrived at West Point "earning the highest grades of any cadet since Robert E. Lee."[431] In World War I, he led the respected 42nd Division into the German lines at Cote de Chatillon.[432] As a result of his heroic efforts, he earned seven Silver Stars.[433] General MacArthur's future was bright as a result of his many accomplishments. After the Great War, he would go on to hold a number of influential jobs. In 1919, for example, General MacArthur "was appointed commander of the Military District of Manila."[434] And in 1925, General MacArthur "was promoted to major general — the youngest man, at forty-three, to hold that rank."[435] Then, in 1929 General MacArthur would be named Commander of the Philippine Department.[436] In 1930, President Hoover selected General MacArthur to be Army Chief

---

[429]   Mark Perry, *The Most Dangerous Man in America* (New York: Basic Books, 2014), xvii.
[430]   Perry, *The Most Dangerous Man in America*, xi.
[431]   Ibid.
[432]   Ibid.
[433]   Ibid.
[434]   Ibid., xii.
[435]   Ibid.
[436]   Ibid.

of Staff.[437] Simply put, General MacArthur's ascendency into the upper crust of leadership within the U.S. military was breathtaking.

Despite these accomplishments, General MacArthur did have flaws and, above all, enemies, which would cripple him and his desire to amass more power. He was vain and an egomaniac, willing to go to great lengths to extend his power and influence. During the Great War, General MacArthur "wore his command cap jauntily to one side, went into battle armed only with a cane, and wrapped himself in a flowing silk scarf."[438] The quintessential prima donna of the U.S. military. General MacArthur's attire was indicative of his narcissism, ego and "my way or the highway" approach to leadership. His clothing revealed a strong sense of self, unbridled swagger and unapologetic confidence. General MacArthur believed he answered to no one, at least he thought he did.

General MacArthur believed in himself, almost to a fault. The General enjoyed the spotlight and cherished praise. He relished opportunities to gain adoration from others. As William Manchester eloquently put it in *American Caesar*, "In a word, he was vain. Like every other creature of vanity, he convinced himself that his drives were in fact selfless."[439] His self-worth was tied to his patriotism. General MacArthur's unbending loyalty to the United States was an expression of his ego.

---

[437]   Ibid.

[438]   Ibid.

[439]   William Manchester, *American Caesar: Douglas MacArthur 1880 – 1964* (New York: Little Brown and Company, 1978), 9.

The General's huge ego both helped and hurt his career. He expected to win, and he often did. At a reunion of his World War I Rainbow Division in 1935, General MacArthur quoted Dionysius: "It is a law of nature, common to all mankind, which time shall neither annul nor destroy, that those who have greater strength and power shall bear rule over those who have less."[440] He expected not only to win, but also to dominate those around him who had less power than himself. Sitting at the top of the mountain, he had trouble appreciating the rivers and streams, trees and bushes, as they were all just a hazy blur to him. Put another way, General MacArthur was too removed from the struggle of African-Americans and the poor to comprehend their misery or, for that matter, care about their hardships.

The General's narcissistic style of leadership smothered his humanity, making it virtually impossible for him to empathize with the plight of African-American soldiers. Like an individual suffering from cloudy vision from cataracts, General MacArthur's pride made it difficult for him to comprehend how racism was, in fact, a huge problem in the U.S. military during the Korean War. Consequently, when Marshall was preparing to investigate the court-martials, General MacArthur refused permission for him to travel to Tokyo to talk with the prisoners.[441] The General was adamant racism did not play a role in the disproportionate number of court-martials African-American soldiers faced. As he bluntly put it,

---

[440] Manchester, *American Caesar: Douglas MacArthur 1880 – 1964*, 9.

[441] Thurgood Marshall, "Summary Justice – The Negro GI in Korea," *The Crisis*, May 1951, 297 – 298.

"Not the slightest evidence exists here of discrimination as alleged. As I think you know in this command there is no slightest bias of its various members because of race, color or other distinguishing characteristics."[442] Despite General MacArthur's stonewalling tactics, Marshall and the NAACP would not give up hope.

In spite of General MacArthur's initial objection to Marshall traveling to Tokyo, the NAACP's strategy of reaching out to him and to President Truman worked. For example, Walter White, a ranking member of the NAACP, told General MacArthur "We are certain you want to see they receive full justice not only because they deserve it, but also to counter inevitable communist propaganda through Asia."[443] White's usage of the threat of communist propaganda resonated with the General. Above all else, General MacArthur did not want to look weak in the face of communism. Eventually, President Truman overturned General MacArthur's veto, and gave the NAACP permission to send Marshall to represent African-American soldiers who were up for court-martial.[444]

When Marshall arrived in Tokyo, he ran into more problems with General MacArthur. Marshall discovered there were no African-American soldiers at the headquarters of Far East Command.[445] When he confronted General MacArthur about the lack of diversity at the U.S. Army of the Far East Headquarters, the General replied, "There is none

[442] Marshall, *Summary Justice – The Negro GI in Korea*, 297 – 298.

[443] "Marshall to Leave for Japan on Jan. 11," *Pittsburg Courier*, January 1951, 4.

[444] Lu Sun, "Battling the Military Jim Crow: Thurgood Marshall and the Racial Politics of the NAACP During the Korean War" MA thesis, Vanderbilt University, 2014), 15.

[445] "Lawyer is Praised as Civil Defender," *New York Times*, April 1951, 27.

qualified."[446] Marshall then replied, "Well, I just talked to a Negro yesterday, a sergeant, who has killed more people with a rifle than anybody in history. And he is not qualified?"[447] General MacArthur replied, "No."[448]

General MacArthur's intransigent stance on race aggravated Marshall. He was angry African-American soldiers were putting their lives on the line for America and yet "were not treated equally even during their military service."[449] This exchange between the two men was just the tip of the iceberg. Marshall would later find institutional racism was deeply interwoven into the U.S. military and, specifically, in the court-martial proceedings.

After Marshall arrived in Tokyo, he immediately got to work, despite running into some hurdles. Some believed he was put under "loose surveillance" by the U.S. military and the U.S. State Department.[450] Nevertheless, Marshall would continue with his mission, determined to discredit the excessive number of court-martials African-American soldiers faced.

Each day Marshall would make a detailed list of things he needed to accomplish. He wrote down on a sheet of paper points which warranted further investigation. These items were then submitted to the Inspector

---

[446]   Marshall, Thurgood. Interviewed by Ed Erwin. April 13th, 1977. transcript, Columbia Center for Oral History, Columbia University. New York, NY.

[447]   Marshall, *Columbia Center for Oral History Interview*

[448]   Ibid.

[449]   Mark Tushnet, *Making Civil Rights Law: Thurgood Marshall and the Supreme Court, 1936 – 1961* (Oxford: Oxford University Press, 1996), 83.

[450]   Tushnet, *Making Civil Rights Law: Thurgood Marshall and the Supreme Court, 1936 – 1961*, 7.

General.[451] Afterward, Marshall would go back and scrutinize statements which "did not quite fit."[452] He looked for inconsistencies in stories and found many. Through his investigations into these first-hand accounts, Marshall found "It was not possible for some of the things they said to be true."[453] He wrote a preliminary report where he highlighted what he found, what he believed to be the cause of the court-martials, and who he believed was to blame for them.[454]

Of the numerous court-martial cases of African-American soldiers, the NAACP decided Lieutenant Leon A. Gilbert, an African-American officer in the 24th who was convicted and sentenced to death, would be given priority. Gilbert's case was at once exceptional and tragic. He "was the Commander of Company A, 24th Infantry Regiment, and his unit occupied the right flank of the regiment's most forward line of resistance."[455] When it appeared North Korean and Chinese forces had broken the line and that he and his soldiers might be cut off from other American forces, Gilbert pulled his men back. "Colonel Horton V. White, the regiment's commanding officer, ordered the soldiers to return to the front. All the enlisted soldiers compiled with the order — except Gilbert, who insisted he was "scared" and could not go back."[456] Colonel White

---

[451] Marshall, Thurgood. Interviewed by Ed Erwin. April 13th, 1977. transcript, Columbia Center for Oral History, Columbia University. New York, NY.

[452] Marshall, *Columbia Center for Oral History Interview*

[453] Ibid.

[454] Ibid.

[455] "Cowardice in Korea? The Trial of Lieutenant Leon A. Gilbert for Misbehavior Before the Enemy," American Bar Association, accessed on August 19, 2020, https://www.americanbar.org/groups/litigation/publications/litigation_journal/2018-19/summer/cowardice-korea-trial-lieutenant-leon-gilbert-misbehavior-the-enemy/.

[456] Ibid.

demanded Gilbert return to the frontline, but he refused. As a result of his insubordination, Gilbert was court-martialed for "misbehavior before the enemy" and for refusing to follow orders from his commanding officer.[457]

Despite Gilbert's defense that he was mentally unstable, he was sentenced to death.[458] Marshall and the NAACP intervened. Marshall argued Gilbert's punishment for dereliction of duty was too excessive. Eventually, President Truman gave in to the pressure and commuted his sentence to twenty years in prison. After serving only five years of his sentence, Gilbert was dismissed from the U.S. Army and freed from jail.

The initial sentence of death Gilbert received was disproportionate to the crime he committed. As a result of Gilbert's case, the large number of African-American soldiers who were court-martialed gained national attention. As a consequence, protests on racial inequality within the U.S. military took place in the United States. Beyond that, the case encouraged "Army lawyers to carefully monitor court-martials coming out of Korea to mitigate excessive sentences."[459] Finally, the NAACP began to take interest in the large number of African-American soldiers who were court-martialed in Korea. With the help of the NAACP, many court-martial cases levied against African-American soldiers would eventually be overturned.

Gilbert's case also had a profound impact on other African-American soldiers who awaited trial. African-American soldiers who were court-martialed followed Gilbert's case closely. Even so, many Afri-

---

457   Ibid.
458   Ibid.
459   Ibid.

can-American soldiers felt helpless. They believed their fate was prede-termined. Marshall would ask the men, "Why didn't you tell your lawyer what really happened? Why didn't you tell the court? Why didn't you tell somebody?"[460] When Marshall pushed them further on the matter, they all gave the same answer: "It was not worth trying. We knew when we went in there we were all going to come out the same way. Each one of us hoped and prayed we would only get life."[461]

Surprisingly, each soldier used the Gilbert case as evidence they would not receive a fair trial. Some African-American soldiers stated, "They gave that officer, Lieutenant Gilbert, death, only because he is a Negro. What did you expect them to give a Negro enlisted man? We know what the score is."[462] The verdict handed down to Gilbert sent a shockwave throughout the ranks of African-American soldiers who were awaiting trial. The message was simple. You do not matter. Your fate is preordained, so why stand up for yourself?

Marshall's thorough research uncovered a number of discrepan-cies with the court-martial cases. For example, one GI was convicted of cowardice. However, the soldier who enlisted at the age of fifteen was stationed "in Japan and was sent to Korea ...without revealing his true age because he knew he would have been returned to the United States as a youthful hero rather than permitted to get into the thick of the fight-

---

[460] Marshall, Thurgood. Interviewed by Ed Erwin. April 13th, 1977. transcript, Columbia Center for Oral History, Columbia University. New York, NY.

[461] Marshall, *Columbia Center for Oral History Interview*

[462] Ibid.

ing."[463] Private J.P. Morgan was court-martialed for "alleged violation of the seventy-fifth Article of War and sentenced to ten years of hard labor" for failing to be on duty.[464] Luckily for Morgan, he was able to provide documentation he was in an Army hospital "during the period when he was charged with not being on duty."[465] In other cases, four men were convicted of "misbehavior in the presence of the enemy although they were stationed miles behind the battle line and assigned to mess duty."[466] Marshall discovered a pattern. All of these men were arrested, charged with violation of the seventy-fifth Article of War, convicted and sentenced to twenty-five years in prison. Their convictions were upheld by the 25th Division, but later reversed after being reviewed in Washington.[467]

While the U.S. military was prosecuting and convicting African-American soldiers on weak evidence, it was also letting White soldiers off for similar crimes. One intoxicated White soldier "was assigned to a first aid tent near the front lines."[468] When the White soldier was ordered to come outside of the tent, he ran away and was later found far to the rear. He was tried and convicted to five years in prison. However, his sentence was later reduced to one year in jail.[469] Another White soldier was "given three years for disobedience."[470] One White soldier was found asleep at

---

[463]   Ibid.

[464]   Thurgood Marshall, *Report on Korea* (Washington, D.C.: Library of Congress, 1951), 6.

[465]   Marshall, *Report on Korea*, 6.

[466]   Ibid.

[467]   Ibid., 7.

[468]   Ibid., 8.

[469]   Ibid.

[470]   Ibid.

his sentry post. Yet, he was acquitted of any wrongdoing.[471] A two-tiered system of justice existed within the U.S. military during the Korean War. The penalty White soldiers received for breaking rules differed from the punishments African-American servicemen got for similar crimes. Sadly, White soldiers were less severely punished than African-American soldiers during court-martial proceedings. For White soldiers, the whiteness of their skin protected them from receiving excessive penalties from the U.S. justice system. The inverse was true for African-American soldiers. The skin complexion of African-American soldiers who were court-martialed guaranteed they would not only be punished more harshly, but would also most likely not receive a fair trial.

Racism within the U.S. military justice system also reduced the likelihood African- American soldiers would be given proper representation during the trial. The process was simple. The defendant was "confronted by two officers, who told him they were assigned to serve as his counsel."[472] Then, the defendant was told, "You are allowed to choose your own counsel if there is anyone you prefer."[473] Next, the defendant would place a request for a person to be his legal counsel, but would oftentimes be denied. Finally, a backup counsel was provided to the defendant.

The quality of the backup counsel given to African-American soldiers on trial was questionable at best. "In numerous instances the

---

[471]   Ibid.

[472]   Marshall, Thurgood. Interviewed by Ed Erwin. April 13th, 1977. transcript, Columbia Center for Oral History, Columbia University Libraries. New York, NY.

[473]   Marshall, *Columbia Center for Oral History Interview*

counsel spent no more than fifteen or twenty minutes with the men about to be tried."[474] In some instances, men were pulled from foxholes, told to get dressed and taken to Pusan to conduct a court-martial case. Since many of these men did not want to jeopardize their careers, they did not question the insufficient time they were given to prepare for the case.[475] They just followed orders. Thus, the counsels' lack of preparation for court-martial trials decreased the likelihood they would make a compelling enough argument which would get their clients' court-martial cases overturned.

Providing African-American soldiers with proper legal representation was an afterthought for the U.S. military. As Marshall put it, "They were denied free choice of counsel, they were hastily tried without adequate opportunity to consult with their legal defense."[476] Without proper counsel, African-American soldiers could not effectively defend themselves before a court of law. To add insult to injury, "charges were levied against African-American soldiers by officers who had contempt for them and they were tried before other officers of the same ilk."[477] In other words, racist officers who did not want to serve alongside African-American soldiers frequently manufactured charges against them so they would be court-martialed. Once charged, racist prosecutors built their cases on questionable evidence. Then, African-American soldiers

---

[474] Ibid.

[475] Ibid.

[476] Thurgood Marshall, *Report on Korea* (Washington, D.C.: Library of Congress, 1951), 12.

[477] Marshall, *Report on Korea*, 12.

were given counsel ill-prepared to fight on their behalf in court. Finally, an all-White jury usually found them guilty which sealed their fate. The U.S. military justice system became a kind of meat grinder for African-American soldiers. It chewed them up and spit them out. The entire court-martial process was rigged.

To Marshall, most court-martials African-American soldiers faced were less about the U.S. military justice system rendering a fair verdict and more about creating the illusion justice was being served. The racial composition of court-martial proceedings ensured a fair trial would not take place. "All the commanding officers who approved charges were White. The entire staff of the Inspector General's office and of the trial Judge Advocate's office were one hundred percent White?"[478] To hide the inherent bias generated by having an all-White staff at the Inspector General's office, White commanding officers had the audacity to add one African-American serviceman to each of the staffs at the Inspector General's office one week before Marshall came for a visit.[479] Tokenism at its finest. African-American servicemen who were added to the staffs of the Inspector General's office served to create the perception the justice system in the U.S. military was fair, just and equitable. This, however, could not be further from the truth. The Inspector General's office was complicit in maintaining a system which was inherently racist and averse to change.

---

[478] Ibid., 138.
[479] Ibid.

The ethnic composition of the Inspector General's staff directly impacted the outcomes of the court-martial trials. For example, in total sixty African-American soldiers were sentenced compared to two White soldiers.[480] If you dig deeper into the numbers, the disparity in terms of the severity of the sentences becomes even more noticeable. One African-American was sentenced to death while no Whites were sentenced to death.[481] Fifteen African-Americans were sentenced to life in prison while no Whites were sentenced to life in prison.[482] One African-American was sentenced to fifty years in prison while no Whites were sentenced to fifty years in prison.[483] Seven African-Americans were sentenced to ten years in prison while no Whites were sentenced to ten years in prison.[484] Only two White soldiers received sentences. One White soldier was sentenced to five years in prison, while another White soldier received three years.[485] The data speaks for itself.

Additionally, the speed of the actual court-martial trials gave the proceedings a formulaic, rushed quality which hindered a real verdict from being reached. "In four cases the trials which sentenced men to life imprisonment ran forty-two minutes, forty-four minutes, and the other two for fifty minutes each."[486] The legal proceedings of a court-martial happened within a short timeframe. First, the court-martial board read

---

[480]   Ibid.
[481]   Ibid.
[482]   Ibid.
[483]   Ibid.
[484]   Ibid.
[485]   Ibid.
[486]   Ibid., 139.

the charges and then swore in witnesses. Next, trial and defense counsels scrutinized the evidence. The legal counsels then made their arguments. Afterward, the court-martial board read the rights of the defendant from the court-martial manual. Then, the court took a brief recess. After a brief discussion on the case by the court-martial board, a ruling was declared. If the soldier was found guilty, the defendant's sentence was read before the court.[487]

Given the speed at which the court-martials took place, a fair and just verdict could not be reached. As Marshall eloquently put it, "Even in Mississippi a Negro will get a trial longer than forty-two minutes, if he is fortunate enough to be brought to trial."[488] All of these factors combined meant court-martial trials for African-American soldiers were, in reality, not trials at all. They were political theater, designed to give the false impression justice was being served.

While this is troubling on a number of different levels, inequality within the court-martial system could have been prevented if General MacArthur intervened. The Air Force and Navy did not have a considerable number of court-martials of African-American soldiers. Integration was done in a more systematic, equitable manner within the Air Force and Navy. In the Army, things were different. Instead of embracing President Truman's Executive Order 9981, which desegregated the U.S. military, General MacArthur sought to undermine it. General MacArthur

---

[487]   Ibid.
[488]   Ibid.

wanted to maintain old, outdated U.S. military procedures as they related to race. The General refused to take the necessary steps to ensure African-American soldiers were treated fairly within the U.S. military justice system. Instead, he prioritized winning the war. Protecting the rights of African-American soldiers was an afterthought.

Marshall, however, challenged General MacArthur's commitment to integration. His investigation amounted to an indictment of the court-martial proceedings during the Korean War and, above all, a critique on General MacArthur's leadership. Through Marshall's findings, he discovered General MacArthur did not seek to create an environment where African-American soldiers and White soldiers would be treated as equals within the U.S. military. Rather, General MacArthur reaffirmed the existence of deeply entrenched racism and bias within the U.S. military. Consequently, African-American soldiers during the Korean War were left vulnerable. Lacking the proper resources and the right skin color to combat an attack on their creditability, African-American soldiers were susceptible to unwarranted attacks which would tarnish their reputations.

Marshall, however, changed that dynamic. His investigation of the court-martials of African-American soldiers uncovered evidence which delegitimized the verdicts reached in many of the cases. Miraculously, Marshall single-handedly protected the reputations of many African-American soldiers serving in the 24th by getting most of their court-martials either thrown out or getting their sentences reduced.

Marshall fought for and, ultimately, secured justice for many African-American soldiers unjustly court-martialed in Korea. Taking on the State Department, U.S. Army and General MacArthur, Thurgood Marshall emerged as a true American hero. A champion of restorative justice.

CHAPTER 5

Impact

Lieutenant Tom Hudner and President Truman walked onto the porch. The crowd applauded. Approximately three hundred people packed themselves into the Rose Garden. President Truman grinned at the crowd. He wore a gray suit and a red tie. As always, the commander-in-chief looked neat, clean and well put together. Meanwhile, Hudner scanned the crowd and saw Daisy, Ensign Jesse Brown's wife. She looked at him and smiled. Daisy was holding a bouquet of red roses. Finally, President Truman looked over at Hudner and said, "Shall we!" President Truman descended the stairs while Hudner and his family followed along. [489]

President Truman walked over to the microphone and said, "The President of the United States takes pleasure in presenting the Medal of Honor to Lieutenant Thomas Hudner Jr., U.S. Navy."[490] A roar of applause erupted from the crowd. After the crowd quieted down, President Truman

---

[489]   Adam Makos, *Devotion* (New York: Ballantine Books, 2015), 389 – 392.

[490]   Makos, *Devotion*, 389 – 392.

gave a brief summary of Hudner's heroics. He spoke of how Hudner crash-landed on a mountain to help save his friend and shipmate, Ensign Brown.

President Truman stated, "Lieutenant Hudner's exceptionally valiant action and selfless devotion to a shipmate sustain and enhance the highest traditions of the U.S. Naval Service."[491] Generals, admirals and other U.S. military personnel looked on with approval. After the speech, President Truman picked up a felt-covered box from the podium and opened it. He reached inside the box and pulled out a bronze, star-shaped Medal of Honor. President Truman said, "You earned this." Then he said, "This is the greatest honor anyone can get." President Truman took the medal and draped it around the neck of Hudner.[492] Next, cameramen took a few pictures of President Truman with Hudner. Before they could take their pictures, President Truman said, "Mrs. Brown, would you be willing to join Lieutenant Hudner and me?"[493] Daisy nodded and joined the President and Hudner. The three of them took pictures together. As the cameramen were taking their pictures, President Truman said, "Okay! Get your shots, movie men."[494]

Brown and Hudner's story of friendship, devotion and sacrifice is noteworthy. The story highlights Brown's commitment to becoming the first African-American Navy fighter pilot. It marks the slow, arduous process of integrating the U.S. military. And it shows the blossoming of a

---

[491]   Ibid.
[492]   Ibid.
[493]   Ibid.
[494]   Ibid.

genuine friendship between the two men. On a deeper level, Brown's story paints a false narrative of racial reconciliation between African-American and White soldiers.

Even so, the Korean War did change the lives of ordinary African-American soldiers. Some were left with emotional scars from traumatic experiences they lived through during the war. A number of African-American soldiers found a career in the U.S. military, while others were able to finance a good education paid for by the U.S. military. Still, others experienced a change in their economic status. Some African-American soldiers gained access to jobs and training which would have otherwise been inaccessible. Thus, the Korean War became a double-edged sword for African-American veterans. It gave some a key they used to unlock a bright future, while leaving others with mental illness which would plague them for the rest of their lives.

For some African-American soldiers, the Korean War eased their transition into lucrative careers in education and business. Others used their experiences as a springboard for social activism. Yet for others, the war continues to torment. For this group of veterans, the war negatively impacted their mental health, their relationships with their family, and their outlook on political life. Ironically, the war also injected into them a new sense of purpose in life by opening up new opportunities. Like a morning swim on a hot summer day, the Korean War jump-started the lives of countless African-American soldiers, paving the way for many bright futures.

One way the Korean War helped African-American soldiers develop a renewed sense of self was with military jobs available to them. According to Michael Green's *Black Yanks in the Pacific,* "enlistment remained the most direct way to take advantage of militarization opportunities."[495] In other words, signing up for the U.S. military gave African-American soldiers job security. An African-American veteran from South Carolina, for example, stated, "being a sharecropper and a farmer, I had no other way of going in life."[496] He eventually served in the U.S. military for two decades.[497] Books like Kimberley Phillips's *War: What Is It Good For?* reveal that an African-American's choice to join the military during the Korean War was largely a pragmatic decision. After the war, many African-American soldiers struggled to find work.[498] "This overwhelmingly young, male, and frequently underemployed population viewed the military as a means to earn regular wages, better their education, and acquire new job training and skills."[499] Phillips suggests some African-Americans

---

[495] Michael Green, *Black Yanks in the Pacific,* (Ithaca: Cornell University Press, 2010), 137.

[496] Green, *Black Yanks in the Pacific,* 137. *Black Yanks in the Pacific* later uses statistics to support its claim that African-American participation in the U.S. armed forces went up after the Korean War. According to the book, "More than one in ten soldiers was black. The trend outlasted Vietnam and the draft; in 1984, 20 percent of those serving in the military were African-Americans" (141-142). Other books like *The Double V* by Rawn James suggest that African-American enlistment after the Korean War went up significantly. According to James, roughly sixty years after Executive Order 9981, "one third of all senior enlisted personnel, 11 percent of officers, and 7 percent of generals and admirals" are African-American (240).

[497] Ibid.

[498] Kimberley Phillips, *War: What Is It Good For?* (Chapel Hill: University of North Carolina Press, 2012), 151.

[499] Phillips, *War: What Is It Good For?*, 151. Books like Richard Stillman's *Integration of the Negro in the U.S. Armed Forces* indicate that working for the U.S. military was a good job for many Afri-

viewed the military as a way to enhance their quality of life by giving them access to education and employment. Simply put, the military provided soldiers with a steady paycheck and social mobility. With this paycheck, they could provide housing for themselves, could get married and raise families.

Beyond providing a steady paycheck, the U.S. military also helped African-American soldiers get an education. For many African-American veterans, access to more educational opportunities minimized the impact structural racism had on their ability to secure economic independence. Porche Taylor, for example, earned three degrees—a BS, MS, and Ph.D—all paid for by the U.S. military.[500] Harold Brown received his Ph.D from Ohio State University, also paid for by the military. As he explained, "When I finished my last hour of my last dissertation with my Ph.D is when I ran exactly out of money. I used every dime."[501] Eugene Lloyd similarly took advantage of the GI Bill, which paid for his college degree from Tennessee State University.[502] Some veterans, like Roy Dell Johnson, a Korean War veteran who was wounded several times, took advantage of the rehabilitation program to get an education. According to Johnson, "I did not have to pay for anything, like if I needed a computer, we did not

---

can-American soldiers. For example, Army Sergeant First Class John Lawrence stated, "A lot of us Negroes never had it so good. A corporal can make $1,000 by re-enlisting, buy a car and live big. The young Negro in uniform feels big in it. It shows he's an American and that he's as good as anyone else" (57-48).

[500] Porche Taylor. Interviewed by Eliot Pope. Personal Interview. Richmond, Virginia, December 22, 2014.

[501] Harold Brown. Interviewed by Rebecca Wiggenhorn. Personal Interview. Beavercreek, Ohio, May 15, 2010.

[502] Eugene Lloyd. Interviewed by Eliot Pope. Personal Interview. Chicago, Illinois, February 13, 2015.

have computers then, but if I needed one, I could get one."[503] The educational opportunities provided to African-American soldiers who served in the U.S. military during the Korean War forever changed their lives.

Education helped African-American soldiers in a variety of ways. First, with an education, they gained important skills they could leverage in the workforce. These skills helped them compete for better-paying jobs. Secondly, education provided African-American soldiers with a sense of accomplishment which undoubtedly increased their confidence. Finally, education provided these veterans with a chance to build their social and professional networks. Through their social and professional networks, they were able to secure job interviews and share knowledge which could further their careers.

Along with African-American Korean War veterans getting access to free education, veterans from the war received more job opportunities. Some soldiers, for example, stayed in the military and moved up the ranks to increase their status, get a larger paycheck, secure healthcare, and to access retirement benefits. According to Taylor, "You do something to get decorated. You spend your time in. It comes."[504] Taylor insinuated that the longer a soldier stayed in the Army the more likely he or she would move up the ranks. In Taylor's case, he served during World War II, the Korean War, and the Vietnam War and quickly moved up the ranks. In

---

[503] Roy Dell Johnson. Interviewed by Eliot Pope. Personal Interview. Arlington, Texas, March 2, 2015.
[504] Porche Taylor. Interviewed by Eliot Pope. Personal Interview. Richmond, Virginia, December 22, 2014.

the end, Taylor retired as the first African-American to become a full colonel in the U.S. Army.

The economic benefits of military service during the Korean War were not limited to those soldiers willing to become "lifers." Although some African-American soldiers made a career of the U.S. military, others became teachers in the Reserve Officer Training Corps (ROTC).[505] When John Thomas got out of the service, he went to teach ROTC at Fort Knox.[506] From there, he went on to work in ROTC at Attucks High School in Indianapolis, Indiana in 1978, and finally finished his career teaching ROTC at Arlington High School, also located in Indianapolis, Indiana in 1995.[507] In total, Thomas served in the military for twenty-eight years and taught for an additional twenty years. Other veterans found work at jobs which were earmarked specifically for veterans. Jesse Jenkins, for instance, worked as a molder in a foundry.[508] He then worked for thirty-seven years in the Veterans Administration Office as a food service worker and a butcher.[509] Finally, he was a chief of building management service at LA's Service Cargo.[510] In each of these roles, Jenkins got the job based, at least in part, on his veteran status.[511]

---

[505] John Thomas. Interviewed by Brianna Brooks. Personal Interview. Indianapolis, Indiana, October 4, 2009.

[506] Ibid.

[507] Ibid.

[508] Jesse Jenkins. Interviewed by Eliot Pope. Personal Interview. Crown Point, Indiana, February 18, 2015.

[509] Ibid.

[510] Ibid.

[511] Ibid.

When African-American soldiers arrived home, their outlook on life changed. Following service in a technically desegregated military, they came home to a country which was still segregated. The invisible wall which separated African-Americans and Whites was still firmly intact. African-American soldiers were still required to ride in the back of buses, drink from separate water fountains, and send their children to segregated schools. This disrespect did not resonate well with some African-American Korean War veterans as they were taught to stand up for themselves. Many felt betrayed. Others were angry. Some soldiers believed they had served their country honorably, but were still treated poorly. Some soldiers looked for ways to address the injustices of Jim Crow.

For many veterans, the war raised their social consciousness by alerting them to social and political inequalities throughout the world. Men like Curtis Morrow became more aware of the struggle for freedom waged by people of color during his time in Korea.[512] According to Morrow, while he was stationed in Japan he had a conversation with a fellow soldier about Africans in Libya fighting for their independence from British rule.[513] The conversation left an impression on Morrow. When he got back to the States after his deployment, he desired to learn more about revolutionary movements taking place around the world. When Morrow learned Kwame Nkrumah, a revolutionary in Ghana, was looking for African-Americans to help rebuild Africa while enrolled as

---

[512]   Curtis Morrow. Interviewed by Eliot Pope. Personal Interview. Chicago, Illinois, January 7th, 2015.
[513]   Ibid.

an art student at the American Academy of Art, Morrow immediately signed up.[514] Leaving school, he joined the movement to overthrow the British government in Ghana. Morrow lived in the West African country for over ten years.[515] Hence, the war inspired some African-Americans to engage actively in social justice issues or go so far as to participate in revolutionary movements, as Morrow did.

While the war did not transform every African-American Korean War veteran into a revolutionary, the Korean War did leave a lasting impression on how they interacted with other people. The war helped some learn how to negotiate with others. William Anderson's experiences during the Korean War taught him how to live with other people. As Anderson put it, "Like I told you, all these nuts I used to be with — well, one time this nut may be the guy that keeps you — that saves your life, so you learn to live with people. You learn to get along with people."[516]

---

[514]   Ibid.

[515]   Ibid. When Curtis Morrow came home, he became disillusioned with America. Dr. Martin Luther King, Jr., and other civil rights leaders were endorsing a nonviolent approach to combating racial injustice. Morrow questioned King's tactics. As Morrow put it, "Non-violence? Is he kidding? We thought it was a trap set, a booby trap or something, leading people in, trying to ambush." The civil rights movement, according to Morrow, did not want African-American veterans from the Korean War. "No soldier, especially combat soldier, would be invited to participate in the march in Selma," he claimed. African-American soldiers were viewed as a liability to the civil rights movement. Because they were trained to respond to violence with violence, Morrow believed the civil rights movement thought leaving African-American soldiers out of nonviolent protests — which could easily turn violent at the hands of white police or anti-civil rights activists — was the best course of action. While the nonviolent, centrist part of the civil rights movement failed to appeal to him, Morrow related to the extremist element within the civil rights movement: the Nation of Islam. Through his interaction with the Nation of Islam, Morrow became more self-aware and gave up smoking and drinking. In fact, Morrow befriended Minister Louis Farrakhan, the leader of the Nation of Islam, then and now, while he was exploring his relationship with the civil rights movement. Morrow credits Farrakhan for inspiring his social awakening. According to Morrow, Farrakhan was "a smart, good dude. Great brother, man, and so in the evenings, we would sit around and talk about our situation, the world situation. That was when I first became aware of politics."

[516]   William Anderson, Jr. Interviewed by Mary Brandes. Personal Interview. Madison, Wisconsin, August 27, 2009.

Thus, the experiences of some U.S. soldiers during the war helped them gain the ability to be more accepting of others. Ironically, some African-American soldiers became less confrontational and more amicable as a result of the war.

Just as the Korean War helped some African-American soldiers become more tolerant of others, the war also helped some of them in their personal lives and professional careers. For some soldiers like A.J. Nero, the war made them more mature.[517] As he put it, "I had grown up a couple of years" as a result of the war.[518] Some African-American veterans, like Jeanne Beasley, suggested they became more physically active after the war. According to Beasley, "I think I have much more stamina."[519] In fact, other women at her job at a hospital would ask her to do extra tasks because they viewed her as having more energy than they did. Thus, one overlooked effect of the Korean War was it made some African-American veterans of the war more responsible and enthusiastic workers.

Unfortunately, the Korean War's impact on African-American soldiers was not entirely positive. Although the Korean War made some African-American soldiers' better collaborators and more adaptive and energetic in the workplace, others reported becoming cynical about people as a result of the war. For example, Clarence Senor believed the war made him mistrust people. As Senor put it, "My wife says, 'You do not

---

[517] A.J. Nero. Interviewed by Eliot Pope. Personal Interview. Chicago, Illinois, November 14, 2014.

[518] Ibid.

[519] Jeanne Beasley. Interviewed by William Browne. Personal Interview. National Harbor, Maryland, August 7, 2009.

like anybody, do you?' I said, 'No. What I do not like is what people say and what people do.'"[520] When Senor was questioned further about this point, he clarified, "I do not try to judge them. They judge themselves."[521] In other words, Senor validated his criticism of others by suggesting their poor behavior spoke for itself. Consequently, the Korean War made Senor skeptical of people and their intentions.

Not only did the war make some African-American veterans more cynical towards people, but also the social consciousness they got from the war made some of them suspicious of the concept of war. For example, Harold Brown believed the U.S. government was intervening in wars the country should not be involved in.[522] He believed America's foreign policy should be more isolationist and less engaged in the social and political affairs of other sovereign nations. While Brown did concede the U.S. government needed a strong military, he also indicated the country should initially use statesmanship to resolve problems before resorting to war.[523]

Brown's belief that the United States should exhaust diplomacy before opting to go to war is similar to Homer Franklin's pacifist position on war. According to Franklin, the Korean War "gave me a long standing, I guess, sense of awareness and concern about the futility of war, particu-

---

[520] Clarence Senor. Interviewed by Mark DePue. Personal Interview. Springfield, Illinois, November 5, 2008.

[521] Ibid.

[522] Harold Brown. Interviewed by Rebecca Wiggenhorn. Personal Interview. Beavercreek, Ohio, May 15, 2010.

[523] Ibid.

larly that war."[524] Additionally, Franklin believed none of the goals of the Korean War aligned with the interest of the people of the United States. He could not "see any real value to the people of this country from the war."[525] Hence, Franklin's distaste for war was a direct result of his participation in the Korean War. His inability to see how the Korean War benefited U.S. citizens made him conclude war as a general principle was a waste of time, energy, and money. Hence, Brown and Franklin's experiences in the Korean War gave them insight into the futility and wastefulness of war.

The emotional impact of the war on those who survived cannot be overstated. Most soldiers lost friends and comrades in combat, and many almost lost their own lives. Such traumatic events would stay with them for the rest of their lives. The psychological impact of the war manifested itself in their dreams. For example, James Lacy's dreams helped him reconnect, in a way, with some of his comrades who were killed during the Korean War. As Lacy put it, "I still have dreams, and I still fight. I still fight."[526] Lacy stated in one dream he saw a big, long wall which paralleled a street he was walking along.[527] As he walked down the street, he heard a voice say, "Hey Jimmy! Jimmy!"[528] He looked over at the wall and heard the same voice say, "Over here Jimmy."[529] When he went over to the wall, he spotted all of his old friends who were killed in the Korean

---

[524]   Homer Franklin. Interviewed by Eliot Pope. Personal Interview. Chicago, Illinois, November 28, 2014.

[525]   Ibid.

[526]   James Lacy. Interviewed by Eliot Pope. Personal Interview. Chicago, Illinois, January 20, 2015.

[527]   Ibid.

[528]   Ibid.

[529]   Ibid.

War, including one friend in particular, Rusty Lewis.[530] In his dream, Lacy said to Lewis, "I thought you guys got killed."[531] Lewis responded, "No. What we did, they took us and put us in this wall. We play basketball. We play football."[532] The deceased soldier added, "We climb up on the fields." Lacy continued, "and he says, 'See Sergeant Don on the end?' I say, 'Yeah.' He says, 'He's going to call us and tell us OK.'"[533] Lacy's dream reveals the psychological impact the Korean War had on his psyche: more than fifty years after the conflict, Lacy continues to mourn the loss of his friends, strives to remember them as having fun by playing football and basketball together, and wishes to reconnect with them.

Not all African-American Korean War veterans had dreams which helped them frame their lost friends from the war in a positive light. Some African-American soldiers, in fact, had dreams which tormented them. Lieutenant Colonel Bussey's dreams evoked strong emotions that frightened him. According to Colonel Bussey, "At night I went back to the killing floor, and it was ugly, very ugly."[534] When he lay on his back, he dreamt of Chinese soldiers running over his shallow grave.[535] These soldiers bruised his ribs, and their feet stuffed sand in his nose, making it difficult for him to breath.[536] During these dreams, Colonel Bussey would

---

[530]   Ibid.

[531]   Ibid.

[532]   Ibid.

[533]   Ibid.

[534]   Charles Bussey, *Firefight at Yechon: Courage and Racism in the Korean War* (Washington: Macmillan Publishing, 1991), 259 - 260.

[535]   Bussey, *Firefight at Yechon: Courage and Racism in the Korean War*, 259 – 260.

[536]   Ibid.

turn over in his sleep and cover his face. He would often sweat through his bedclothes and yell out in fear.[537] As a result of these dreams, he could often only sleep for three or four hours at a time.[538] For Colonel Bussey, his dreams revealed the depth of the war's psychological impact on him as they forced him to relive the horrors of war each night.

For some African-American soldiers, the war's impact is not only revealed in their dreams but also in their response to various types of weather conditions. James Williams, for example, did not like it when it was snowing because it reminded him of his experiences in combat in Korea.[539] Rainy, stormy weather conditions also had an adverse effect on Williams. Inclement weather reminded him of his first night in Korea when there was "a firefight way off, way off in the mountains. You could see the little things, looked like a firefly, you know what I mean?"[540] When Williams asked a fellow soldier what they were seeing, someone told him "There is a firefight going on down there." [541] Williams then heard rumbling and saw flashes and concluded it was about to rain. However, he was wrong. It was not thunder and lighting, but artillery shells going off.[542] As Williams witnessed this nighttime firefight, he was told, "You will get used to that; you will not pay it no mind."[543] Williams unfortunately never got used to the sounds of war. These visual and auditory representations

---

[537]   Ibid.
[538]   Ibid.
[539]   James Williams. Interviewed by Eliot Pope. Personal Interview. Chicago, Illinois, January 12, 2015.
[540]   Ibid.
[541]   Ibid.
[542]   Ibid.
[543]   Ibid.

of war would affect him for many years to come. He would continue to react negatively to precipitation and loud weather conditions.

Hearing the rumbles and blasts and seeing flashes of light of combat in the Korean War left a deep scar on Williams's psyche. He consequently became sensitive to thunderstorms and was eventually diagnosed with post-traumatic stress disorder.[544] Williams described an incident where a natural weather pattern entirely overwhelmed his senses. He described an average Sunday evening when he was having a drink at home with his girlfriend when it started to rain.[545] While it was still just raining, he converted the couch to a bed and went to sleep. However, when thunder and lightning began, Williams rolled off the sofa and stayed on the floor for ten to fifteen minutes.[546]

Williams's girlfriend started laughing at him, prompting him to ask, "What is so damn funny?"[547] She said, "The way you was carrying on. I thought you were fighting the war over again."[548] He responded, "I was, and it is not funny either."[549] Hence, for Williams, as for other veterans, the sights and sounds reminiscent of war could haunt some veterans for

---

[544]   Ibid. Curtis Morrow. Interviewed by Eliot Pope. Personal Interview. Chicago, Illinois, January 7th, 2015. Morrow, who suffered from Post Traumatic Stress Disorder, indicated in his interview that the term was not used during the Korean War to describe his psychological issues from combat. Instead, he suggests the doctors called what he suffered from "battle fatigue." Morrow later revealed in his oral history testimony that he believes the average soldier suffers from Post Traumatic Stress Disorder, but most do not talk about it because "things can be taken out of context." Morrow added that a soldier willing to discuss his experience would most likely disclose his experiences to another soldier because they would be the only listener able to relate.

[545]   Ibid.

[546]   Ibid.

[547]   Ibid.

[548]   Ibid.

[549]   Ibid.

decades. Even something so quotidian as weather conditions had the ability to trigger emotional breakdowns which would transport soldiers like Williams back to the battlefields of Korea.

The emotional trauma soldiers like Williams faced when he returned to the United States required medical attention. The U.S. military treated the emotional trauma soldiers experienced after the war in a variety of ways. When Roy Dell Johnson was discharged from the U.S. military, he was "locked down for five months."[550] After the war, Johnson would sit mute and stare off into space.[551] Johnson was eventually diagnosed with schizophrenia.[552] To treat his condition, he was administered electric shock, insulin, and hydrotherapy. For electric shock therapy, electrodes were attached to his head while two men held his torso and two other men held his legs. Then, a doctor held his head back, put a mouthpiece on him, and proceeded to shock him. Fortunately, the insulin and hydrotherapy Johnson received were less traumatic. He was given insulin which made him go to sleep, and later given glucose which brought him back to consciousness.[553] Hydrotherapy consisted of a man "with a big hose like a fire hydrant that shot cold water" on him.[554] Johnson's experiences after the Korean War exposes the peculiar ways the U.S. military attempted to treat soldiers who suffered from emotional trauma.

---

[550] Roy Dell Johnson. Interviewed by Eliot Pope. Personal Interview. Arlington, Texas, March 2, 2015.
[551] Ibid.
[552] Ibid.
[553] Ibid.
[554] Ibid.

That said, the emotional impact of the Korean War was not limited to their own psyches. Some African-American Korean War veterans suggest the war had a negative impact on their family lives as well. Colonel Bussey, for example, had trouble connecting with his daughter when he got back from the war. After he returned to the States, his daughter, who was eight months old when he left for the war, did not initially recognize him. As he put it, "She referred to me as 'that man,' but time took care of that."[555] Eventually, Colonel Bussey's daughter began to recognize him, and he was able to reestablish a meaningful relationship with her.

War not only affected some soldiers' relationships with their children, but it also damaged some soldiers' relationships with their wives. When Colonel Bussey got back to the United States, he desired to be back fighting in the Korean War.[556] He preferred to be engaged in combat with North Korean and Chinese soldiers, not stuck at home with his wife. As he put it, "I identified more with being out there, where my problems whatever they were, were mine alone and disturbed no one else."[557] Sadly, the horrific sights, pungent smells and chaotic sounds of war became normalized for Colonel Bussey. As a consequence, the battlefields of Korea became a home away from home for the Colonel. Although he made it back alive from the war, his mind was still trapped in the violence and

---

[555] Charles Bussey, *Firefight at Yechon: Courage and Racism in the Korean War* (Washington: Macmillan Publishing, 1991), 259.

[556] Bussey, *Firefight at Yechon: Courage and Racism in the Korean War*, 260.

[557] Ibid.

blood which colored his experiences and he struggled to adapt to civilian life.[558]

One issue Colonel Bussey identified was his need for someone to listen to the atrocities he took part in and witnessed. He thought his wife would be the ideal candidate for this role, but she was unwilling or unable to listen to him. "My wife could not deal with the blood and gore which haunted me. She wanted to hear nothing of killing, maiming, frostbite, barbed wire, fear, trembling, doubt, arson, exhaustion, death, or blood—none of it," Colonel Bussey reflected.[559] Therefore, the Korean War put a strain on Colonel Bussey's marriage because his wife could not accommodate the emotional needs of her husband and he could not find another outlet to express himself.

When James Lacy got back from the Korean War, he tried to reestablish stability in his life. He got married and had three children.[560] Despite this, Lacy was unable to put his Korean War experiences behind him. Like Colonel Bussey, Lacy attempted to talk to his wife about his wartime experiences. As in Colonel Bussey's situation, Lacy's wife refused to listen to him. Lacy's inability to connect with his wife about his wartime experiences strained his marriage.

Lacy and Colonel Bussey's traumatic experiences during the Korean War draws attention to the ways in which the wives of some African-American soldiers were ill- equipped to help their husbands

---

[558]   Ibid.
[559]   Ibid.
[560]   James Lacy. Interviewed by Eliot Pope. Personal Interview. Chicago, Illinois, January 20, 2015.

overcome the emotional trauma of military service. Simply put, the war impacted both veterans and their families, adding stress to marriages and distance between fathers and their children.

While the Korean War had an emotional impact on African-American veterans, the war more often than not transformed the men who served in a positive way. The war made them stronger, more resilient. It gave them an opportunity to develop their minds by getting an education. At school, they learned skills which would provide greater opportunities for them within the marketplace. New jobs were also created for African-American Korean War veterans which they otherwise would not have been qualified to get. Good-paying jobs African-American soldiers were now able to access changed their lives. They made more money. They expanded their social network. They could move into better communities which had better schools their children could attend. In effect, it gave them a greater sense of self-worth and a new interpretative lens by which to view the world. With a new sense of purpose, African-American veterans of the Korean War would go on to push for change in America. They would stand up to racism. They would be the foot soldiers of the civil rights movement who would force America to take the demands of African-Americans fighting for equal rights seriously. Just as the Korean War changed these soldiers, they changed America.

CHAPTER 6

Perception

Ensign Jesse Brown was an American hero. Through his bravery and fortitude, he overcame insurmountable odds to become the first African-American naval aviator. Even though he died in battle, his legacy paved the way for other African-Americans who would later serve in the U.S. military. All African-American soldiers owe a debt of gratitude to Brown and his military exploits.

In spite of Brown's heroic yet tragic story, controversy still exists regarding how African-American soldiers during the Korean War are portrayed within history. In 1996, a large uproar came from African-American Korean War veterans from the 24th Infantry regarding the publication of William Bowers, William Hammond, and George MacGarrigle's *Black Soldier, White Army,* a book which aimed to address why the all-Black 24th was disbanded. They were angry and frustrated. They threatened to take legal action against the Pentagon if it published an official history describing the failures of the all-Black 24th. They believed the 24th was "a scapegoat for the overall failures of the U.S. Army in the early days of the Korean war."[561]

The effort to sue the Pentagon was lead by David Carlisle, a member of the engineering squadron who served alongside the 24th and a West Point graduate. Carlisle said, "The 24th performed as well as, and accomplished at least as many outstanding combat successes as, other U.S. regiments."[562] Carlisle's point is clear. William Bowers, William Hammond, and George MacGarrigle distorted the contributions the 24th made to the Korean War effort. He believed the 24th served honorably during the Korean War, and he wanted to set the record straight.

Carlisle did not stop at praising the 24th's performance on the battlefield. He would go on to attack William Bowers, William Hammond, and George MacGarrigle, the Army historians who wrote *Black Soldier, White Army*. As Carlisle put it, "Army historians continue misleadingly and insultingly to characterize the regiment's combat performance."[563] In other words, William Bowers, William Hammond, and George MacGarrigle manipulated the narrative of the 24th's participation in the Korean War in a way that made the fighting unit look incompetent, even though evidence exists which suggest otherwise. Later, Carlisle insinuated the U.S. Army let the men of the 24th down by indicating they were "being libeled by the Army that they not only served, but that they fought and

---

[561]   Philip Shenon, "Veterans of Black Unit Threaten Suit Over Army's Account of Their Service," *The New York Times*, May 7th, 1996, 2. https://timesmachine.nytimes.com/timesmachine/1996/05/07/029912.html?pageNumber=16.

[562]   Shenon, "Black Veterans Sue," 3.

[563]   Ibid.

died for."[564] Carlisle was seeking to redeem the honor and glory of the 24th, and in doing so the legacy of all African-Americans who served during the Korean War.

In the end, Carlisle's efforts to stop William Bowers, William Hammond, and George MacGarrigle's *Black Soldier, White Army* from being published failed. The book would go on to become an important yet controversial history book on the 24th. Yet, Carlisle was successful in helping to create doubt about the validity of the claim the 24th did not meet the expectations of the U.S. military. As one African-American Korean War veteran put it, "They say we were cowards. But I saw no cowards. I fought as much as anybody else. I just do not understand how they can say this about us."[565] Prominent historian Clay Blair, author of the book entitled *The Forgotten War*, echoed similar sentiments. Blair argued many Army units performed poorly during the beginning stages of the Korean War "and the bottom line is the 24th did not do any worse."[566] In other words, all American infantry units struggled against seasoned Chinese and North Korean soldiers at the start of the war.

The 24th was a convenient scapegoat. Because it was an all-Black unit which was destined to be broken up as a result of Executive Order 9981, it was used by many within the military community to justify why the entire U.S. Armed Forces suffered numerous defeats against battle-hardened enemy combatants. While the battle over how the 24th is viewed

---

[564] Ibid., 3.
[565] Ibid., 5.
[566] Ibid., 4.

within historiography took place over twenty years ago, problems still exist regarding how the African-American experience during the Korean War is represented. Some historians have whitewashed the history of African-American soldiers during the Korean War by suggesting a real, genuine racial reconciliation took place, even though corroborating evidence that reaffirms this point is thin. Instead, *Forgotten Struggles: African-Americans Confront Racism During the Korean War Era* argues something more compelling took place right before, during and after the war — a more assertive African-American community, willing to take on racial inequality in an unapologetic way, emerged.

Even though Executive Order 9981 was passed before the Korean War began, the role African-American soldiers would play in the U.S. military was not predetermined. Yes, Executive Order 9981 brought an end to discrimination against one's race, creed or color within the U.S. military, but President Truman's executive order was still just a piece of paper. The order meant nothing unless the leaders within the U.S. military believed in the concepts embedded within the document. Real integration could only occur if the hearts and minds of White servicemen changed.

Despite Executive Order 9981, it is safe to conclude many powerful White military commanders still had reservations about African-American soldiers serving alongside White soldiers in the U.S. military. Lieutenant General Almond, General MacArthur and other White servicemen who were against African-American soldiers engaging in armed combat against enemy combatants would have been handed a key victory if the validity of the court-martials African-American soldiers faced were not brought into question. Within this historical context, Thurgood Marshall's successful efforts to either overturn or discredit court-martials African-American soldiers faced is magnified. Marshall's work did more than remove a stain on the legacy of the 24th within the U.S. military. It ensured a political firestorm on the role African-American soldiers should play within the U.S. military was avoided. In order for the slow, delicate process of desegregating the U.S. military to continue, the creditability of the court-martials African-American soldiers faced had to be undermined. If left unchallenged, the court-martials of African-American soldiers could have been used as evidence to suggest desegregating the U.S. military was not in the best interest of this revered American institution. Under these circumstances, the U.S. military could have reverted back to "separate but equal."

In many ways, the Korean War era was like a stained-glass window. Up close the war does not look like much, just a chaotic, bloody series of battles over the span of a few years of fighting with no victor emerging from the war. Dead and wounded soldiers, the establishment of the 38th parallel between North and South Korea and an armistice between the two countries is all that came from the Korean War. On the domestic front, Asa Randolph's efforts to desegregate the U.S. military is often neglected within historiography. And, Marshall's fight to overturn court-martials is an important but overlooked story in his celebrated legal career. While these stories are interesting, they seem to be random historical threads that do not appear to be directly connected with one another.

In reality, these stories are inextricably linked. The enactment of Executive Order 9981, which theoretically desegregated the U.S. military, was dependent upon the success of negotiations which took place between President Truman and Asa Randolph. After President Truman issued Executive Order 9981, the U.S. military gradually shifted towards training African-American soldiers to fight against North Korean and Chinese troops. This change in military policy most likely encouraged Lieutenant Dawkins not to completely slam the door on Jesse Brown's dream of becoming a naval aviator. As a result, Brown took advantage of this change in military policy on race to pry the door open to the exclusive all-White male fraternity of elite naval aviators. Likewise, Curtis Morrow, James Williams, James Lacy and other African-American soldiers would not have had an opportunity to engage in combat during the Korean War if Executive Order 9981 was not enacted. Due to Executive Order 9981, African-American soldiers were now given a chance to prove they were just as loyal, just as brave, just as determined as their fellow White soldiers to help America secure victory. And, if Executive Order 9981 was not issued, Thurgood Marshall would have been robbed of an opportunity to indict the U.S. military justice system as he challenged the legitimacy of court-martials some African-American soldiers faced. When you take a step back and consider all these events as a collective whole, the various colors that comprise the stained-glass window called the Korean War era is brought into focus. It is only then that the Korean War era's significance is fully appreciated.

Within historiography, the Korean War is akin to a neglected step-child. Its bigger, more popular siblings, World War II and the Vietnam War, have been covered extensively by historians. Thousands of books and hundreds of thousands of articles have been written about both wars, while far fewer books and articles about the Korean War have been written. As a consequence, the Korean War often gets overlooked by academics and the general public. Despite that, the Korean War is arguably just as important as World War II and the Vietnam War in history. And, if viewed within the context of the civil rights movement, the Korean War may have been more instrumental in helping the African-American community achieve justice and equality within American society juxtaposed to World War II or the Vietnam War.

Future civil rights activist, including Dr. Martin Luther King, Jr., drew inspiration from Randolph's numerous civil rights victories. The famous March on Washington in 1963, a watershed moment within the civil rights movement highlighted by Dr. Martin Luther King's famous "I Have a Dream" speech, may not have taken place if not for Randolph's threat to march in Washington in 1944. The Korean War also had an impact on the most important legal scholar of the 20th century - Thurgood Marshall. Marshall's success in getting a number of court-martials African-American soldiers faced overturned built his confidence.

After the Korean War, he would later go on to successfully win *Brown vs. Board of Education*, which found racial segregation in schools unconstitutional. Later, he was nominated by President Lyndon Johnson to serve on the U.S. Supreme Court. After being approved by the Senate, Marshall became the first African-American to serve on America's highest, most prestigious court.

The struggles the African-American community experienced during the Korean War era provide lessons on how the community should address the challenges it faces today. The deaths of Breonna Taylor, Ahmaud Arbery, George Floyd, Trayvon Martin, Sandra Bland, Michael Brown and countless others by law enforcement officers indicates the African-American community is vulnerable to unsolicited attacks. More recently, the mass shooting of African-Americans in Buffalo, New York at a Tops supermarket by a White nationalist reaffirms this point. Our lives are often not valued. Our contributions to American society are frequently ignored. Our culture is not appreciated. With the inequality gap widening between African-Americans and Whites in education, health care, and housing, African-Americans are being robbed of opportunities and resources which could enhance their quality of life.

Yet, there is hope. The resolve, determination and commitment to excellence highlighted by individuals such as Curtis Morrow, Asa Randolph, Thurgood Marshall, Ensign Jesse Brown and others provide a blueprint on how the African-American community can overcome the obstacles it is currently experiencing today. As White nationalist ideology continues to spread online unabated, we must assume things will get worse before they get better. We must accept the fact that there will be more racially motivated shootings which will take place at mosques, synagogues, churches, grocery stores, schools, and malls. All marginalized groups are at risk.

Given the African-American community's unique relationship with the United States, we are more than capable of weathering the thunderstorms which are gathering on the horizon. We can and we will survive. Our dogged determination, grit and ingenuity will win the day. To prepare for the challenges we will undoubtedly confront in the near future, we must consolidate resources, strengthen the bonds which connect us to one another and strive for excellence in academia, business, finance, and the sciences. Beyond that, we must honor our commitment to help other marginalized communities. We have a moral obligation to help our Latin-American, Jewish-American, Asian-American, Muslim-American and LBGTQ brothers and sisters as they confront various forms of extremism.

In the face of insurmountable odds, the African-American community emerged victorious during the Korean War era. Within this short period in time in which the Korean War was fought, are lessons our ancestors left for us to draw strength from. The application of these kernels of knowledge to the challenges we face today will lead us to a brighter future. Our destiny is in our hands.

BIBLIOGRAPHY

Abner, Alan. *Psywarriors: Psychological warfare during the Korean War.* Shippensburg: Burd Street Press, 2001.

Acheson, Dean. *The Korean War.* New York: Norton, 1971.

Adam, Clarence. *An American Dream: The Life of an African American Soldier and POW Who Spent Twelve Years in Communist China,* Amherst: University of Massachusetts Press, 2007.

Alexander, Bevin. *Korea: The First War We Lost.* New York: Hippocrene Books, 1986.

Anderson, Carol. *Eyes Off the Prize: The United Nations and the African American Struggle for Human Rights, 1944 – 1955.* New York: Cambridge University Press, 2003.

Anderson, Jervis. *A. Philip Randolph – A Biographical Portrait.* Berkeley: University of California Press, 1986.

Apel, Otto. *MASH: An Army Surgeon in Korea.* Lexington: University Press of Kentucky, 1998.

Appleman, Roy E., LTC, AUS (Ret). *East Chosin: Entrapment and Break-out, 1950.* College Station, TX: Texas A and M University Press, 1991.

Arnesen, Eric. *Brotherhoods of Color: Black Railroad Workers and the Struggle for Equality.* Cambridge: Harvard University Press, 2001.

Astor, Gerald. *The Right to Fight: A History of African Americans in the Military.* Novato, CA: Presidio Press, 1998.

Baker, Anni P. *American Soldiers Overseas: The Global Military Presence.* Westport: Prager, 2004.

Baker, Vernon, with Ken Olsen. *Lasting Valor.* Columbus, MS: Genesis Press, 1997.

Baldovi, Louis, ed. *A Foxhole View: Personal Accounts of Hawaii's Korean War Veterans.* Honolulu: University of Hawaii Press, 2002.

Bates, Beth Tompkins. *Pullman Porters and the Rise of Protest Politics in Black America, 1925 – 1945.* Chapel Hill: University of North Carolina Press, 2001.

Berger, Carl. *The Korea Knot, A Military Political History.* Philadelphia: University of Pennsylvania Press, 1964.

Berry, Henry. *Hey, Mac, where ya been? Living Memories of the U.S. Marines in the Korean War.* New York: St. Martin's Press, 1988.

Black, Robert, Col., AUS (Ret). *Rangers in Korea*. New York: Ivy Books, Random House, Inc., 1989.

Blair, Clay. *The Forgotten War: America in Korea 1950-1953*. New York: Times Books, 1987.

Blomstedt, Larry. *Truman, Congress, and Korea: The Politics of America's First Undeclared War*. Lexington: The University Press of Kentucky, 2016.

Bogart, Leo. *Social Research and the Desegregation of the U.S. Army*. Chicago: Markham Publishing Company, 1969.

Booker, Bryan. *African Americans in the United States Army in World War II*. Jefferson: McFarland and Company, Inc., Publishers, 2008

Borstelmann, Thomas. *The Cold War and the Color Line: American Race Relations in the Global Arena*. Cambridge: Harvard University Press, 2001.

Bowers, William and William Hammond and George MacGarrigle. *The 24th Infantry Regiment in Korea*. Washington: Center of Military History, 1996.

Brady, James. *The Coldest War: A Memoir of Korea*. New York: Orion Books, 1990.

Branch, Taylor. *Parting the Waters: America in the King years, 1954 – 1963*. New York: Touchstone, 1988.

Breuer, William. *Shadow Warriors: The Covert War in Korea*. New York: John Wiley & Sons, 1996.

Buckley, Gail. *American Patriots: The Story of Blacks in the Military from the Revolution to Desert Storm*. New York: Random House Trade Paperbacks, 2001

Bussey, Charles. *Firefight at Yechon*. Washington: MacMillan, 1991.

Bynum, Cornelius. *A. Philip Randolph and the Struggle for Civil Rights* (Chicago: University of Illinois Press, 2010.

Caponi-Tabery, Gena. *Jump for Joy: Jazz, Basketball and Black Culture in 1930s America* (Amherst: University of Massachusetts Press, 2008), 36.

Capozzola, Christopher. *Uncle Sam Wants You: World War I and the Making of the Modern American Citizen*. Oxford: Oxford University Press, 2008.

Carter, Allene, and Robert Allen. *Honoring Sergeant Carter: Redeeming A Black World War II Legacy*. New York: Harper Collins Publishing, 2003.

Casey, Steven. *Selling the Korean War: Propaganda, Politics, and Public Opinion in the United States*. Oxford: Oxford University Press, 2008.

Center of Military History, Department of Army. *KOREA-1950*. Washington, DC: Superintendent of Documents, U.S. Government Printing Office, 1989.

Chateauvert, Melina. *Marching Together: Women of the Brotherhood of Sleeping Car Porters*. Urbana: University of Illinois Press, 1997.

Chen, Jian. *Mao's China and the Cold War*. Chapel Hill: The University of North Carolina Press, 2001.

Chinnery, Philip. *Korean Atrocity: Forgotten War Crimes*. Annapolis: Naval Institute Press, 2000.

Cho, Grace. *Haunting the Korean Diaspora Shame, Secrecy, and the Forgotten War*. Minneapolis: University of Minnesota Press, 2008.

Choi, Suhi. *Embattled Memories: Contested Meanings in Korean War Memorials*. Reno: University of Nevada Press, 2014.

Clark, Mark. *Calculated Risk*. New York: Harper and Brothers, 1950.

Clay, Blair. *The Forgotten War: America in Korea 1950 – 1953*. New York: Random House, Inc., 1987.

Colley, David. *Blood for Dignity: The Story of the First Integrated Combat Unit in the U.S. Army*. New York: St. Martin's Griffin, 2003.

Crane, Conrad. *American Airpower Strategy in Korea*. Lawrence: University Press of Kansas, 2000.

Cummings, Bruce. *The Korean War: A History*. New York: Modern Library, 2010.

Cummings, Bruce. *The Origins of the Korean War: Liberation and the Emergence of Separate Regimes, 1945 – 1947*. Princeton: Princeton University Press, 1981.

Dalfiume, Richard. *Desegregation of the U.S. Armed Forces: Fighting on Two Fronts, 1939 – 1953*. Columbia: University of Missouri Press, 1969.

Dannenmaier, William. *We were Innocents: An Infantryman in Korea*. Urbana: University of Illinois Press, 1999.

Daugherty, Leo J. *Train Wreckers and Ghost Killers: Allied Marines in the Korean War*. Washington: U.S. Marine Corps Historical Center, 2003.

Donaldson, Gary. *America at War Since 1945: Politics and Diplomacy in Korea, Vietnam, and the Gulf War*. Westport: Praeger, 1996.

Donnelly, William. *Under Army Orders: The Army National Guard during the Korean War*. College Station: Texas A & M University Press, 2001.

Donovan, Robert. *Nemesis: Truman and Johnson in the Coils of War in Asia*. New York: St. Martin's – Marek, 1984.

Dudziak, Mary. *Cold War Civil Rights: Race and the Image of American Democracy*. Princeton: Princeton University Press, 2001.

Dvorchak, Robert. *Battle for Korea: The Associated Press History of the Korean Conflict*. Conshohocken: Combined Books, 1993.

Edgar, Roy. *South to the Naktong, North to the Yalu*. Washington: Office of the Chief of Military History, 1961.

Edwards, Paul M. *A Guide to Films on the Korean War*. Westport, CT: Greenwood Press, 1997.

Edwards, Paul M. *The Pusan Perimeter, Korea, 1950: An Annotated Bibliography*. Westport, CT: Greenwood Press, 1993.

Egerton, Douglas R. *Death or Liberty: African Americans and the Revolutionary America*. Oxford: Oxford University Press, 2009.

Fehrenbach, T.R. *This Kind of War*. New York: Macmillian, 1963.

Foner, Jack D. *Blacks and the Military in American History: A New Perspective*. New York: Praeger, 1974.

Fontaine, Andre. *History of the Cold War, from the October Revolution to the Korean War, 1917 – 1950*. New York: Pantheon Books, 1968.

Gardner, Lloyd. *The Korean War*. New York: Quadrangle Books, 1972.

Gardner, Michael. *Harry Truman and Civil Rights: Moral Courage and Political Risks*. Carbondale: Southern Illinois University Press, 2002.

Geselbracht, Raymond H. *The Civil Rights Legacy of Harry S. Truman*. Kirksville: Truman State University Press, 2007.

Giangreco, D.M. *War in Korea, 1950 – 1953*. Novato: Presido, 1990.

Goldman, Eric F. *The Crucial Decade: America, 1945 – 1955*. New York: Alfred A. Knopf, 1956.

Green, Michael. *Black Yanks in the Pacific: Race in the Making of American Military Empire after World War II*. Ithaca: Cornell University Press, 2010.

Greenberg, Cheryl *To Ask for an Equal Chance: African Americans in the Great Depression*. Lanham: Rowman & Littlefield Publishers, 2009.

Greene, Robert E. *Black Defenders of America, 1775 – 1973*. Chicago: Johnson Publishers, 1974.

Gropman, Alan. *The Air Force Integrates: 1945 – 1964*. Washington: Smithsonian Institution Press, 1998.

Gugeler, Russell. *Combat Actions in Korea*. Washington: Office of the Chief of Military History, 1970.

Gye-Dong. Kim. *Foreign Intervention in Korea*. Brookfield: Dartmouth Pub. Co., 1993.

Halberstam, David. *The Coldest Winter: America and the Korean War*. Hyperion: New York, 2007.

Halliday, Jon, and Bruce Cummings. *Korea: The Unknown War*. New York: Pantheon Books, 1998.

Harris, William. *Keeping the Faith: A. Philip Randolph, Milton P. Webster, and the Brotherhood of Sleeping Car Porters, 1925 – 1937*. Urbana: University of Illinois Press, 1977.

Hasting, Max. *The Korean War*. New York: Simon and Schuster, 1987.

Heinl, Robert. *Victory at High Tide; The Inchon – Seoul Campaign*. Philadelphia: Lippincott, 1968.

Hickey, Michael. *The Korean War: The West Confronts Communism*. Woodstock: Overlook Press, 2000.

Hickman, Bert. *The Korean War and United States Economic Activity*. New York: National Bureau of Economic Research, 1955.

Higgins, Trumbull. *Korea and the Fall of MacArthur: A Precis in Limited War*. New York: Oxford University Press, 1960.

Hinshaw, Arned. *Heartbreak Ridge: Korea, 1951*. New York: Praeger, 1989.

Hoare, James. *Conflict in Korea: An Encyclopedia*. Santa Barbara: ABC – CLIO, 1999.

Hogan, Michael J. *A Cross of Iron: Harry S. Truman and the Origins of the National Security State, 1945 – 1954*. New York: Cambridge University Press, 1998.

Holmes, Richard. *Acts of War: The Behavior of Men in Battle*. New York: Simon and Schuster, 1985.

Holober, Frank. *Raiders of the China Coast: CIA Covert Operations during the Korean War*. Annapolis: Naval Institute Press, 1999.

Jager, Sheila Miyoshi. *Brothers at War: The Unending Conflict in Korea*. New York: W.W. Norton & Company, 2013.

James, Rawn Jr. *The Double V: How Wars, Protest, and Harry Truman Desegregated America's Military* New York: Bloomsbury Press, 2013.

Jian, Chen. *China's Road to the Korean War: The Making of the Sino – American Confrontation*. New York: Columbia University Press, 1994.

Kaufman, Burton. *The Korean Conflict*. Wesport: Greenwood Press, 1999.

Kaufman, Burton. *The Korean War: Challenges in Crisis, Credibility, and Command*. New York: McGraw – Hill Companies, 1997.

Kersten, Andrew and Clarence Lang, eds. *Reframing Randolph: Labor, Black Freedom, and Legacies of A. Philip Randolph*. New York: New York University Press, 2015.

Knauer, Christine. *Let Us Fight as Free Men*. Philadelphia: University of Pennsylvania Press, 2014.

Knott, Richard. *Attack from the Sky: Naval Air Operations in the Korean War*. Washington: Naval Historical Center, 2004.

Kukla, Barbara. *Swing City: Newark Nightlife 1925 – 1950*. Philadelphia: Temple University Press, 1991.

Lee, Steven. *The Korean War*. New York: Longman, 2001.

Lee, Suk Bok. *The Impact of U.S. Forces in Korea*. Washington: National Defense University Press, 1987.

Li, Xiaobing. *Mao's Generals Remember Korea*. Lawrence: University Press of Kansas, 2001.

Lipsitz, George. *A Life in Struggle: Ivory Perry and the Culture of Opposition*, rev. ed. Philadelphia: Temple University Press, 1995.

Lowe, Peter. *The Korean War*. New York: Palgrave Paperback, 2000.

MacDonald, C.A. *Korea, The War Before Vietnam*. New York: Free Press, 1987.

MacGregor, Morris J., Jr. *Defense Studies Series: Integration of the Armed Forces, 1940 – 1965*. Washington: Center of Military History, 1981.

MacIntyre, William. *Colored Soldiers*. Macon: Burke, 1923.

Mahoney, Kevin. *Formidable Enemies: The North Korean and Chinese Soldier in the Korean War*. Novato: Presidio, 2001.

Mandelbaum, David. *Soldier Groups and Negro Soldiers*. Oakland: University of California Press, 1952.

McCoy, Donald and Richard Ruetten. *Quest and Response: Minority Rights and the Truman Administration*. Lawrence: University Press of Kansas, 1973.

McFarland, Keith. *The Korean War: An Annotated Bibliography*. New York: Routledge, 2010.

McWilliams, Bill. *On Hallowed Ground: The Last Battle for Pork Chop Hill*. Annapolis: Naval Institute Press, 2004.

Melady, John. *Korea Canada's Forgotten War*. Toronto: Dundurn Press, 2011.

Merrill, John. *Korea: The Peninsular Origins of the War*. Newark: University of Delaware Press, 1989.

Mershon, Sherie, and Ron Powers. *Foxholes and Color Lines: Desegregating the U.S. Armed Forces*. Baltimore: Johns Hopkins University Press, 2002.

Middleton, Harry. *The Compact History of the Korean War*. New York: Hawthorn Books, 1965.

Miller, Ruth Thompson, Joe R. Feagin, Leslie H. Picca, *Jim Crow's Legacy: The Lasting Impact of Segregation*. New York: Rowman and Littlefield, 2015.

Millett, Allan. *The War for Korea, 1945 – 1950: A House Burning*. Lawrence: University Press of Kansas, 2005.

Millett, Allan. *The War of Korea, 1950 – 1951: They Came from the North*. Lawrence: The University Press of Kansas, 2010.

Mitchell, Arthur. *Understanding the Korean War: the participants, the tactics and the course of conflict.* Jefferson: McFarland & Company, 2013.

Mjagkj, Nina, *Loyalty in the Time of Trial,* Boulder: Rowman and Littlefield Publishers, 2011.

Moeller, Susan. *Shooting War: Photography and the American Experience of Combat.* New York: Basic Books, 1989.

Moore, Christopher. *Fighting for America: Black Soldiers, the Unsung Heroes of World War II.* New York: One World Press, 2005.

Morehouse, Maggi. *Fighting in the Jim Crow Army: Black Men and Women Remember World War II.* New York: Rowman and Littlefield Publishers, Inc. 2000.

Moreno, Paul. *Black Americans and Organized Labor: A New History.* Baton Rouge: Louisiana State University Press, 2006.

Morrow, Curtis. *What's a Commie Ever Done to Black People?* Jefferson: McFarland and Company, 1951.

Myrdal, Gunnar. *An American Dilemma: The Negro Problem and Modern Democracy.* Vol. 2. Rutgers University, NJ: Transaction Publishers, 1996.

Nalty, Bernard and Morris Macbregar. *Blacks in the Military Essential Documents.* New York: Rowman and Littlefield, 1981.

Nalty, Bernard. *Long Passage to Korea: Black Soldiers and the Integration of the U.S. Navy.* Washington: Naval Historical Center, 2003.

Nalty, Bernard. *Strength for the Fight: A History of Black Americans in the Military.* New York: The Free Press, 1986.

Nelson, Dennis D. *The Integration of the Negro into the U.S. Navy.* New York: Octagon Books, reprint, 1982.

Nichols, Lee. *Break Through on the Color Front.* New York: Random House, 1993.

O'Ballance, Edgar. *Korea: 1950 – 1953.* Hamden: Archon Books, 1969.

Osmer, Harold. *U.S. Religious Journalism and the Korean War.* Washington: University Press of America, 1980.

Osur, Alan. *Blacks in the Army Air Force During World War II*, Washington: Office of Air Force History, 1975.

Paige, Glenn. *The Korean Decision, June 24th – 30th, 1950.* New York: Free Press, 1968.

Paschall, Rod. *Witness to War: Korea.* New York: Berkley Pub Group, 1995.

Pearlman, Michael. *Truman & MacArthur Policy, Politics, and the Hunger for Honor and Renown.* Bloomington: Indiana University Press, 2008.

Perks, Robert, and Alistair Thomson, eds. *The Oral History Reader.* New York: Routledge Press, 1998.

Peters, Richard. *Voices from the Korean War: Personal Stories of American, Korean, and Chinese Soldiers.* Lexington: University Press of Kentucky, 2004.

Pfeffer, Paula. *A. Philip Randolph, Pioneer of the Civil Rights Movement,* Baton Rouge: Louisiana State University Press, 1990

Phillips, Kimberley. *War: What Is It Good For?* Chapel Hill: University of North Carolina Press, 2012.

Pierpaoli, Paul. *Truman and Korea: The Political Culture of the Early Cold War.* Columbia: University of Missouri Press, 1999.

Portelli, Alessandro. "What Makes Oral History Different." *The Oral History Reader.* Ed. Robert Perks and Alistair Thomson. New York: Routledge, 1998. 32 – 42.

Posey, Edward. *The U.S. Army's First, Last, and Only All Black Rangers.* New York: Savas Beatie, 2009.

Reed, Allan. *The War for Korea, 1950 – 1951: They Came From the North.* Lawrence: University Press of Kansas, 2010.

Rishell, Lyle. *With a Black Platoon in Combat: A Year in Korea.* College Station: Texas A & M University Press, 1993.

Robinson, Charles. *Dangerous Liaisons: Sex and Love in the Segregated South.* Fayetteville: University of Arkansas Press, 2003.

Rosenberg, Jonathan. *How Far the Promised Land? World Affairs and the American Civil Rights Movement from the First World War to Vietnam.* Princeton: Princeton University Press, 2005.

Schlossman, Steven and Sherie Mershon. *Foxholes and Color Lines Desegregating the U.S. Armed Forces.* Baltimore: John Hopkins University Press, 2007.

Shaw, Henry I., Jr., and Ralph W. Donnelly. *Blacks in the Marine Corps.* Washington: History and Museums Divisions, Headquarters, U.S. Marine Corps, reprint, 1988.

Shogan, Robert. *Harry Truman and the Struggle for Racial Justice.* Lawrence: University of Kansas Press, 2013.

Shrader, Charles. *Communist Logistics in the Korean War.* Westport: Greenwood Press, 1995.

Smith-Lenz, Adriane. *Freedom Struggles: African Americans and World War I.* Cambridge: Harvard University Press, 2009.

Stillman, Richard. *Integration of the Negro in the U.S. Armed Forces.* New York: Frederick A. Praeger, 1968.

Stokesbury, James. *A Short History of the Korean War.* Harper Perennial: New York, 1990.

Stone, I. F. *The Hidden History of the Korean War.* 2nd ed. New York: Monthly Review Press, 1969.

Streissguth, Thomas. *The Korean War*. Mankato: The Childs World, 2015.

Stueck, William. *The Korean War: An International History*. Princeton: Princeton University Press, 1997.

Summers, Harry G. *Korean War Almanac*. New York, NY: Facts on File, 1990.

Thompson, James. *True Colors: 1004 Days as a Prisoner of War*. Port Washington, NY: Ashley Books, 1989.

Thompson, Reginald. *Cry Korea*. London: Macdonald, 1951.

Toland, John. *In Mortal Combat: Korea, 1950 – 1953*. New York: Morrow, 1991.

Truman, Margaret. *Harry S. Truman*. New York: William Morrow, 1972.

Tye, Larry. *Rising from the Rails: Pullman Porters and the Making of the Black Middle Class*. New York: Henry Holt and Company, 2004.

Verney, Kevern. *Black Civil Rights in America*. New York: Routledge, 2000.

Wainstock, Dennis. *Truman, MacArthur, and the Korean War*. Westport: Greenwood Press, 1999.

Watts, Joe C. *Korean Nights: The 4th Ranger Infantry Company (Abn), 1950 – 1951*. St. Petersburg, FL: Southern Heritage Press, 1997.

Weintraub, Stanley. *MacArthur's War: Korea and the Undoing of an American Hero*. New York: Free Press, 2000.

Whelan, Richard. *Drawing the Line: The Korean War, 1950 – 1953*. Boston: Little, Brown, 1990.

Whiting, Allen. *China Crosses the Yalu; The Decision to enter the Korean War*. New York: Macmillian, 1960.

Wilkinson, Allen. *Up Front Korea*. New York: Vantage Press, 1967.

Williams, David. *I Freed Myself: African American Self – Emancipation in the Civil War Era*. Cambridge: University of Cambridge Press, 2014.

Williams, Phil. *Security in Korea: War, Stalemate, and Negotiation*. Boulder: Westview Press, 1994.

Wynn, Neil A. *The African American Experience during World War II*. New York: Rowman and Littlefield Publishers, Inc. 2010.

Young, Charles. *Name, rank, and serial number: Exploiting Korean War POWs at home and board*. New York: Oxford University Press, 2014.

Articles

Boffey, Philip. "Franklin Delano Roosevelt at Harvard." *The Harvard Crimson*, December 13, 2020. https://www.thecrimson.com/article/1957/12/13/franklin-delano-roosevelt-at-harvard-phistorians/.

Borch, Fred. "Cowardice in Korea? The Trial of Lieutenant Leon A. Gilbert for Misbehavior Before the Enemy." *American Bar Association*, August 28, 2020. https://www.americanbar.org/groups/litigation/publications/litigation_journal/2018-19/summer/cowardice-korea-trial-lieutenant-leon-gilbert-misbehavior-the-enemy/.

Carls, Kelsey. ""The Social Evil in Kansas City": Machine Politics And The Red-Light District." *The Kansas City Public Library*, December 28, 2020. https://pendergastkc.org/article/social-evil-kansas-city-machine-politics-and-red-light-district.

Elving, Ron. "'Franklin D. Roosevelt: A Political Life' Examines The Personal Traits That Marked FDR For Greatness." *NPR Book Review*, November 8, 2017. https://www.npr.org/2017/11/08/562251084/franklin-d-roosevelt-a-political-life-examines-the-personal-traits-that-marked-f.

"GIs Convicted in Korea Ask NAACP Aid," *The Chicago Defender*, November 25, 1950.

Jakab, Peter. "Hell's Angels: Hughes' Big Crash and Harlow's Big Break." *Smithsonian: National Air and Space Museum*, December 28, 2020. https://airandspace.si.edu/stories/editorial/hells-angels.

"Jim Crow Laws." *Public Broadcasting Station*, August 25, 2020. https://www.pbs.org/wgbh/americanexperience/features/freedom-riders-jim-crow-laws/.

"Lawyer is Praised as Civil Defender," *New York Times*, April 6, 1951.

Lerch, Sarah. "The Hidden History of Ohio State's Black Student Body." *Ohio State University*, https://odi.osu.edu/hidden-history-ohio-states-black-student-body.

Leuchtenburg, William. "Franklin D. Roosevelt: The American Franchise." *University of Virginia Miller Center*, July 28, 2020. https://millercenter.org/president/fdroosevelt/the-american-franchise.

"Marshall to Leave for Japan on Jan. 11," *Pittsburg Courier*, January 6, 1951.

Marshall, Thurgood. "Summary Justice – The Negro GI in Korea," *The Crisis*, May 1951.

"NAACP Gives GIs Priority." *The Chicago Defender*, December 2, 1950.

Ott, Tim. "How Franklin Roosevelt's Health Affected His Presidency." *Biography*, December 28, 2020. https://www.biography.com/news/franklin-roosevelt-health.

"Pullman Porters." *History*, October 8, 2021. https://www.history.com/topics/black-history/pullman-porters.

Stamp, Jimmy. "Traveling in Style and Comfort: The Pullman Sleeping Car." *Smithsonian Magazine*, December 11, 2013. https://www.smithsonianmag.com/arts-culture/traveling-style-and-comfort-pullman-sleeping-car-180949300/.

"Thurgood Marshall." *History,* July 10, 2020. https://www.history.com/topics/black-history/thurgood-marshall.

"When Did 'Kumbaya' Become Such A Bad Thing?" *National Public Radio*, August 4, 2020. https://www.npr.org/2012/01/13/145059502/when-did-kumbaya-become-such-a-bad-thing.

General Information

Encyclopedia Americana. 25 vols. New York, NY: Americana Corporation, 1970.

Letters

Gibson, Kenneth. Kenneth Gibson to Thelma Gibson, Chicago, IL, May 8, 1945.

Social Media – Short Videos

O'Malley, Terence. "T.J. Pendergast: A Man in Full." Documentary film Tom & Harry: The Boss and the President. Streamed live on October 25th, 2015. YouTube video, 5.28.

https://www.youtube.com/watch?v=FaA3irKc2DQ.

Reynolds, Dean. "Pullman railcars: A detour back through time." CBS Morning News. Streamed live on April 13th, 2014. YouTube video, 5.18. https://www.youtube.com/watch?v=PhZw1tKgxkc.

Newspapers, Magazines, Journals

American Studies

Defender Newspaper

Ebony

Foreign Affairs

Indiana Magazine of History

Jet

Journal of Blacks Studies

Journal of American Studies

L.A. Times

New York Times

OAH Magazine of History

Perspectives on Politics

The Journal of African American History

The Journal of Economic History

The Journal of Politics

Washington Post

Online Forums

Geneva Convention - https://www.icrc.org/applic/ihl/ihl.nsf/ ART/365-570008?OpenDocument

Korean War Project - http://www.koreanwar.org

New Jersey Government - http://www.nj.gov/military/korea/factsheets/
afroamer.html

ROTC Program - http://todaysmilitary.com/training/rotc

U.S. Department of Veterans Affairs -http://www.va.gov/vetdata/docs/
specialreports/kw2000.pdf

Oral History Collections

African American Veterans Oral History Project – Evansville African
American Museum

Columbia Center for Oral History – Columbia University

Dr. Otis Eliot Pope, Jr. Forgotten Soldiers from a Forgotten War Oral
History Archive – Chicago, Illinois

Louie B. Nunn Center for Oral History – University of Kentucky

Roscoe Robinson Papers – Library of Congress

Samuel Proctor Oral History Project – University of Florida

Veterans History Project – Library of Congress

Video Oral History Walter Sanderson – History Makers

Presentations

Seol Woong Lee, "Forestry in Korea" World Forestry Center, (Slideshow presentation, International Fellow, Korea World Forestry Center, Incheon, Korea, 2005). https://www.worldforestry.org/wp-content/uploads/2015/11/korea_s.lee.pdf.

Reports

Black Americans in Defense of Our Nation, Office of the Assistant Secretary of Defense for Civilian Personnel Policy/Equal (Washington: U.S. Government Printing Office, 1990).

Conrad C. Crane, Michael E. Lynch, Shane P. Reilly, Jessica J. Sheets, *U.S. Army Heritage and Education Center, Learning the Lessons of Lethality: The Army's Cycle of Basic Combat Training, 1918 – 2019* (Carlisle: U.S. Army Heritage and Education Center, 2018 – 2019).

U.S. Department of Veterans Affairs: Data on Veterans of The Korean War – Assistant Secretary for Planning and Analysis Office of Program and Data Analyses, United States, U.S. Department of Veterans Affairs, (Washington: U.S. Department of Veterans Affairs, 2000).

Thesis

Sun, Lu. "Battling the Military Jim Crow: Thurgood Marshall and the Racial Politics of the NAACP During the Korean War." Master's thesis, Vanderbilt University, 2014. https://ir.vanderbilt.edu/bitstream/

handle/1803/13201/lusunmasterthesis.pdf?sequence=1&isAl-lowed=y.

Websites

American Federation of Labor and Congress of Industrial Organizations. "A. Philip Randolph." Accessed December 27, 2021. https://aflcio.org/about/history/labor-history-people/asa-philip-randolph.

Asia Society. "The Geography of the Koreas." Accessed on June 22, 2020. https://asiasociety.org/education/geography-koreas.

Climates to Travel. "Climate – South Korea." Accessed on June 23, 2020. https://www.climatestotravel.com/climate/south-korea.

Government of Canada. "Terrain." Accessed April 20, 2020. https://www.veterans.gc.ca/eng/remembrance/history/korean-war/land-morning-calm/conditions/terrain.

HCA Delaware Historical and Cultural Affairs. "African-American Participation During World War I." Accessed July 29, 2021. https://history.delaware.gov/african-americans-ww1/.

History. "March on Washington." Accessed October 29, 2009. https://www.history.com/topics/black-history/march-on-washington.

History Central. "Childhood of FDR." Accessed December 28, 2020. https://www.historycentral.com/FDR/FDRchild.html.

Lemelson – MIT. "George Pullman: Pullman Sleeper Railroad Car." Accessed November 24, 2020. https://lemelson.mit.edu/resources/george-pullman.

National Association for the Advancement of Colored People. "2020 Nation's Premier Civil Rights Organization." Accessed on July 2, 2021. https://naacp.org/nations-premier-civil-rights-organization/.

National Public Radio. "All Things Considered - Former Pullman Porter Subtly Confronted Racism." Accessed December 15, 2021. https://www.npr.org/templates/story/story.php?storyId=103945861.

Ohio State University. "The Hidden History of Ohio State's Black Student Body." Accessed December 28, 2021. https://odi.osu.edu/hidden-history-ohio-states-black-student-body.

Public Broadcasting Service. "Character Above All: Harry S. Truman Essay." Accessed July 25, 2022. https://www.pbs.org/newshour/spc/character/essays/truman.html.

White House. "Franklin Roosevelt." Accessed August 25, 2020. https://www.whitehouse.gov/about-the-white-house/presidents/franklin-d-roosevelt/.

INDEX